THE ANTI-INFLAMMATORY JOURNEY

Discover the Health Benefits, Quick and Easy Recipes, and
Practical Tips for Transitioning to an Anti-Inflammatory Lifestyle

ZARA JIMENEZ

TABLE OF CONTENTS

INTRODUCTION

Welcome to the world of the Anti-Inflammatory Diet for Beginners! If you're taking the first steps on your journey to a healthier lifestyle, you've made a commendable choice. This diet isn't just about losing weight - it's about reducing chronic inflammation, restoring balance to your body, and fostering overall wellness. Inflammation is a natural defense mechanism of our bodies. Nevertheless, persistent inflammation can result in a range of health issues, including diabetes, heart disease, arthritis, and potentially cancer. The anti-inflammatory diet is designed to fight chronic inflammation through the power of nutrition, leading to improved health and a reduced risk of these diseases.

Understanding the Anti-Inflammatory Diet

The anti-inflammatory diet is not a 'diet' in the conventional sense. It is more of a lifestyle, a blueprint for a healthier way of eating. It focuses on incorporating foods known for their anti-inflammatory properties and avoiding those that can trigger inflammation. This diet emphasizes fruits, vegetables, lean proteins, nuts, seeds, and healthy fats, while limiting processed foods, red meats, and sugary drinks.

The Benefits of the Anti-Inflammatory Diet

The advantages of the anti-inflammatory diet go beyond reducing inflammation. It can also promote weight loss, stabilize blood sugar, boost metabolism, and increase your energy levels. Moreover, by focusing on a variety of nutrient-dense foods, this diet can help improve your overall nutrient intake, contributing to better health.

Diving Deeper into the Anti-Inflammatory Diet

The **Complete Anti-Inflammatory Diet for Beginners** guide provides a comprehensive approach to this diet. It includes a 7-day meal plan to help beginners navigate their first week, detailed shopping lists for your grocery trips, and easy-to-follow recipes that are both healthy and delicious. This guide is your ultimate companion for kick-starting your journey with the anti-inflammatory diet.

A Lifestyle Change for Better Health

By adopting the anti-inflammatory diet, you're not just changing the food on your plate, but setting the foundation for a healthier lifestyle. You're taking a proactive step toward reducing inflammation, boosting your immune system, and preventing disease. Whether you're looking for a detox plan like the 21-day anti-inflammatory diet or seeking a long-term dietary change, the resources available can cater to your needs. Improving your health and well-being can be a significant undertaking, but it's important to remember that even the most remarkable achievements start with small, initial steps. The anti-inflammatory diet is a commitment to your overall wellness, and by familiarizing yourself with its principles and potential benefits, you're already making strides towards a healthier lifestyle. This journey of personal transformation can be immensely rewarding, and tackling it with a positive mindset and a willingness to learn can make all the difference. Let's explore this path together and discover the transformative power of the anti-inflammatory diet.

STICK TO A DIET

Sticking with Your Diet: A Guide for Long-Term Success

Sticking to a diet can feel like a constant battle. The temptations are everywhere, and willpower alone can only take you so far. But achieving a healthy relationship with food and creating a sustainable eating pattern is possible. This chapter will equip you with the tools and strategies to navigate the challenges and make your diet a way of life, not just a temporary fix.

Foundational Principles

- **Set Realistic Goals:** Don't aim for overnight transformations. Aim for gradual, achievable milestones that celebrate progress and keep you motivated.
- **Find a Sustainable Diet:** Choose a plan that fits your lifestyle, preferences, and health needs. Restrictive fad diets are difficult to maintain and often lack essential nutrients.
- **Focus on Healthy Habits:** View your diet as a way to nourish your body and fuel your well-being, not just a weight-loss tool.

STRATEGIES FOR SUCCESS

1. Planning and Preparation:

- Meal prep: Dedicate time to prepping healthy meals and snacks for the week to avoid unhealthy choices when pressed for time.
- Grocery shopping list: Plan your meals and create a grocery list to stick to your dietary plan and avoid impulse purchases.

2. Mindful Eating:

- Enjoy the journey, not just the destination. Take your time eating and pay attention to your body's signals so you stop when comfortably full.
- Limit distractions: Put away your phone and focus on the experience of eating.

3. Healthy Snacking:

- Stock your pantry with healthy options to satisfy sudden hunger and avoid grabbing unhealthy snacks.
- Choose fruits, vegetables, nuts, or yogurt for a satisfying and nutritious snack.

4. Temptation Management:

- Identify your triggers: Recognize situations that tempt you to stray from your diet and develop coping mechanisms.
- Don't deprive yourself: Allow yourself occasional treats in moderation to avoid feeling restricted.

5. Support System:

- Find an accountability partner: Share your goals and struggles with a friend or family member for support and motivation.
- Don't underestimate the value of community. Connecting with people on a similar path can offer encouragement and valuable insights.

6. Maintaining Motivation

- **Celebrate Non-Scale Victories:** Acknowledge improvements in your energy levels, mood, and overall well-being, not just weight loss.
- **Focus on Progress, Not Perfection:** There will be slip-ups. Forgive yourself, learn from them, and recommit to your goals.
- **Find Activities You Enjoy:** Incorporate physical activities you find fun into your routine. Exercise shouldn't feel like a chore.

HOW TO START

Understand the Basics of Inflammation

Inflammation is your body's natural immune response to irritation, injury, or infection. While inflammation is a natural healing process, when it becomes chronic and low-grade, it can contribute to various health problems. Learn how diet and lifestyle choices can either promote or reduce inflammation.

Identify Inflammatory Foods to Avoid

Eliminate or minimize consumption of foods that tend to trigger inflammation, such as:

- Refined carbs (white bread, pasta, pastries)
- Fried and processed foods
- Red meat and processed meats
- Sugary and unhealthy-fat-laden foods
- Dairy products (for those sensitive to them)
- Alcohol in excess

Focus on Anti-Inflammatory Foods

Fill your diet with whole, nutrient-dense foods that have anti-inflammatory properties:

- Fruits and vegetables (especially leafy greens, berries, citrus)
- Whole grains (quinoa, brown rice, oats)
- Nuts and seeds
- Fatty fish (salmon, mackerel, sardines)
- Olive oil, avocados, and other healthy fats
- Herbs and spices (turmeric, ginger, garlic, etc.)

Meal Planning and Prep

Stay prepared for busy days by pre-planning meals and cooking healthy dishes in bulk. This helps you stick to the diet and avoid impulse decisions that could derail your progress. Consider using an anti-inflammatory meal planner or cookbook.

Stay Hydrated and Manage Stress

Drink plenty of water throughout the day and find healthy ways to manage stress, such as meditation, yoga, or simply taking time for yourself. Both hydration and stress management are important for reducing inflammation.

Get Enough Sleep and Exercise

Prioritize quality sleep by aiming for 7-9 hours nightly. Research shows insufficient sleep can increase inflammation. Incorporate regular physical activity, including a mix of cardio, strength training, and flexibility work.

Be Patient and Consistent

Transitioning to an anti-inflammatory diet takes time and commitment. Be patient with yourself, and don't get discouraged. Consistency is key to seeing long-term benefits.

THE ADVANTAGES OF AN ANTI-INFLAMMATORY DIET

Inflammation is a natural process in the body's immune response, helping to fight infection and heal injuries. However, chronic, low-grade inflammation is linked to a variety of health problems. This dietary approach prioritizes ingredients that combat inflammation, promoting overall well-being.

Here's a deeper dive into the advantages of incorporating an anti-inflammatory diet into your lifestyle:

1. Reduced Chronic Disease Risk:

- The good news is, you can take control of your health! Chronic, low-level inflammation is linked to a higher risk of heart disease, diabetes, and even some cancers. But here's where diet comes in: an anti-inflammatory eating pattern rich in fruits, vegetables, whole grains, and healthy fats can help shield you from developing these conditions.
- Boost your heart health from the inside out! Fatty fish are champions of omega-3 fatty acids, which studies suggest can reduce inflammation in blood vessels. This translates to a healthier heart for you.

2. Improved Management of Existing Conditions:

- By reducing refined sugars, processed foods, and unhealthy fats, an anti-inflammatory diet can encourage weight loss or healthy weight management. Be mindful of what you ditch, not just what you dish up! Refined sugars, processed foods, and unhealthy fats often pack a double whammy: they're high in calories and can trigger inflammation in the body.

3. Overall Wellbeing Boost:

- Fruits, vegetables, and whole grains take center stage in an anti-inflammatory diet for a reason! They're a powerhouse of essential vitamins, minerals, and antioxidants, all working together to keep your body healthy and inflammation in check. These nutrients can strengthen your immune system, promote healthy digestion, and improve cognitive function.

4. Weight Management:

- By reducing refined sugars, processed foods, and unhealthy fats, an anti-inflammatory diet can encourage weight loss or healthy weight management. These foods are often high in calories and can contribute to inflammation [2].

5. Important to Remember:

While an anti-inflammatory diet offers a multitude of benefits, it's not a quick fix for any health condition. Before diving headfirst into a new diet, especially if you have health concerns, consider a pit stop with a healthcare professional or registered dietician! Think of a healthcare professional or registered dietician as your personal anti-inflammatory guide! They can map out a plan that considers your specific health and preferences, making your journey towards a healthier you a smooth and personalized one.

CHAPTER 1: BREAKFAST RECIPES

OVERNIGHT CHIA PUDDING WITH BERRIES

- Total Time: 8 hours 10 minutes
- Prep Time: 10 minutes
- Servings: 4

Ingredients:

- 1/2 cup chia seeds
- 2 cups unsweetened almond milk
- 2 tablespoons pure maple syrup
- 1 teaspoon vanilla extract
- 1/4 teaspoon ground cinnamon
- 1 cup assorted berries
- 2 tablespoons sliced almonds (optional)

Directions:

1. Whiskchia seeds, almond milk, maple syrup, vanilla, and cinnamon in a medium bowl..
2. Cover the bowl and refrigerate for at least 8 hours or overnight, stirring occasionally, until the mixture has thickened to a pudding-like consistency.
3. Divide the chia pudding evenly among 4 serving bowls or jars.
4. Finish each serving with 1/4 cup mixed berries and sprinkle with sliced almonds, if you like.
5. Serve chilled and enjoy!

Nutritional breakdown per serving:

Calories: 210 kcal, Protein: 6 grams, Carbohydrates: 24 grams, Fat: 10 grams, Saturated Fat: 1 grams, Cholesterol: 0 milligrams, Sodium: 90 milligrams, Fiber: 10 grams, and Sugar: 12 grams.

SPINACH AND FETA FRITTATA

- Total Time: 40 minutes
- Prep Time: 15 minutes
- Servings: 4

Ingredients:

- 8 large eggs
- 1/4 cup unsweetened almond milk
- 1/4 teaspoon ground black pepper
- 1/4 teaspoon salt
- 2 tablespoons extra-virgin olive oil
- 3 cups baby spinach, roughly chopped
- 1 medium onion, diced
- 3 cloves garlic, minced
- 1/2 cup crumbled feta cheese

Directions:

1. Before proceeding, it is crucial to confirm that your oven has been preheated to 375°F (190°C) in order to achieve the best possible outcome.
2. Make the egg mixture: whisk eggs, almond milk, salt, and pepper in a bowl. Set aside.
3. Warm olive oil in a medium nonstick skillet suitable for the oven.
4. Add the onion and sauté for 3-4 minutes, or until translucent.
5. Toss the garlic and spinach into the skillet and cook for another 2-3 minutes, or until the spinach becomes wilted.
6. Gently slide the egg mixture over the spinach and onions in the skillet. Evenly distribute the crumbled feta cheese on top.
7. Pop the skillet in the preheated oven and bake for 18-22 minutes. Aim for a set center and lightly browned edges for the frittata.
8. Take the frittata out of the oven and let it rest for 5 minutes.
9. Slice the frittata into 4 equal portions and serve warm.

Nutritional breakdown per serving:

Calories: 240 kcal, Protein: 18 grams, Carbohydrates: 8 grams, Fat: 16 grams, Saturated Fat: 5 grams, Cholesterol: 345 milligrams, Sodium: 490 milligrams, Fiber: 2 grams, and Sugar: 2 grams.

TURMERIC LATTE

- Total Time: 15 minutes
- Prep Time: 5 minutes
- Servings: 2

Ingredients:

- 2 cups unsweetened almond milk
- 1 tablespoon ground turmeric
- 1 teaspoon ground cinnamon
- 1/2 teaspoon ground ginger
- 1/4 teaspoon ground black pepper
- 1 tablespoon honey or maple syrup (optional)

Directions:

1. Pour almond milk into a small saucepan. Add turmeric, cinnamon, ginger, and a pinch of black pepper. Whisk everything together until well combined.
2. Heat the mixture over medium heat. Stir occasionally and watch for simmering bubbles, which should appear in about 5-7 minutes.
3. Remove the saucepan from the heat. Carefully ladle the fragrant turmeric latte into two mugs.
4. If desired, stir in 1/2 tablespoon of honey or maple syrup per serving to sweeten the latte.
5. Feel free to garnish with a sprinkle of cinnamon or a whole cinnamon stick for an extra layer of flavor.

Nutritional breakdown per serving:

Calories: 90 kcal, Protein: 2 grams, Carbohydrates: 11 grams, Fat: 3 grams, Saturated Fat: 0 grams, Cholesterol: 0 milligrams, Sodium: 55 milligrams, Fiber: 2 grams, and Sugar: 8 grams.

AVOCADO TOAST WITH TOMATO AND BASIL

- Total Time: 15 minutes
- Prep Time: 10 minutes
- Servings: 2

Ingredients:

- 2 slices of whole-grain or sprouted bread
- 1 ripe avocado, halved and mashed
- 1 medium tomato, diced
- 1/4 cup fresh basil leaves, chopped
- 1 tablespoon extra-virgin olive oil
- 1 tablespoon balsamic glaze (or balsamic vinegar)
- 1/4 teaspoon red pepper flakes (optional)
- Salt & pepper to taste

Directions:

1. Heat the bread slices until they have a warm, inviting look.
2. Grab a fork and mash the avocado in a small bowl. Keep going until it has the consistency you want.
3. Divide the mashed avocado evenly between the two pieces of toast, spreading it out to the edges.
4. Top each slice of avocado toast with the diced tomatoes and chopped basil leaves.
5. Drizzle the olive oil and balsamic glaze (or vinegar) over the top of the toasts.
6. For a spicy twist, add red pepper flakes (they're optional). Season to taste with salt and pepper.
7. Serve the avocado toast immediately, while the bread is still warm.

Nutritional breakdown per serving:

Calories: 270 kcal, Protein: 6 grams, Carbohydrates: 21 grams, Fat: 18 grams, Saturated Fat: 2.5 grams, Cholesterol: 0 milligrams, Sodium: 280 milligrams, Fiber: 8 grams, and Sugar: 3 grams.

QUINOA PORRIDGE WITH TOASTED NUTS AND HONEY

- Total Time: 25 minutes
- Prep Time: 10 minutes
- Servings: 4

Ingredients:

- 1 cup uncooked quinoa, rinsed
- 3 cups unsweetened almond milk
- 1 tablespoon ground cinnamon
- 1 teaspoon ground ginger
- 1/4 teaspoon ground cardamom
- 1/4 teaspoon ground nutmeg
- 2 tablespoons honey, plus more for drizzling
- 1/4 cup chopped raw almonds
- 1/4 cup chopped walnuts
- 1/4 cup chopped pecans
- 2 tablespoons unsweetened shredded coconut
- Fresh berries, for serving (optional)

Directions:

1. Pour the rinsed quinoa and almond milk into a medium pot. Increase the heat to medium-high and let it come to a rolling boil.
2. Let it boil, then turn down the heat to low. Let it simmer, covered, for 15-18 minutes. The quinoa is ready when it's tender and most of the liquid has been absorbed.
3. Let the cooked quinoa cool slightly off the heat. Then, fold in the cinnamon, ginger, cardamom, nutmeg, and honey for a flavorful twist.
4. For a toasty crunch, heat up a small skillet over medium heat. Add the chopped almonds, walnuts, and pecans. Cook for 2-3 minutes, stirring frequently, until they're fragrant and have a light brown color.
5. Divide the quinoa porridge among four serving bowls. Top each serving with the toasted nuts and shredded coconut.
6. Drizzle additional honey over the top of the porridge, if desired.
7. Serve the quinoa porridge warm, optionally with fresh berries on the side.

Nutritional breakdown per serving:

Calories: 350 kcal, Protein: 10 grams, Carbohydrates: 40 grams, Fat: 18 grams, Saturated Fat: 3 grams, Cholesterol: 0 milligrams, Sodium: 70 milligrams, Fiber: 7 grams, and Sugar: 12 grams.

GREEN SMOOTHIE WITH KALE, PINEAPPLE, AND GINGER

- Total Time: 10 minutes
- Prep Time: 10 minutes
- Servings: 2

Ingredients:

- 2 cups packed kale leaves, stems removed
- 1 cup frozen pineapple chunks
- 1 cup unsweetened almond milk
- 1/2 cup plain Greek yogurt
- 1 tablespoon freshly grated ginger
- 1 tablespoon honey (optional)
- 1/4 teaspoon ground cinnamon
- 1/4 teaspoon ground turmeric
- Pinch of ground black pepper

Directions:

1. In a high-speed blender, combine the kale leaves, frozen pineapple chunks, almond milk, Greek yogurt, grated ginger, honey (if using), cinnamon, turmeric, and black pepper.
2. Blend everything together on high speed for 1-2 minutes, aiming for a restaurant-quality smoothness.
3. Scrape down the sides of the blender as needed to ensure all the ingredients are well incorporated.
4. Pour the green smoothie into two serving glasses.
5. For the freshest taste, drink your smoothie immediately. Enjoy your smoothie fresh, but leftovers will stay delicious for up to 2 days in the fridge.

Nutritional breakdown per serving:

Calories: 170 kcal, Protein: 10 grams, Carbohydrates: 27 grams, Fat: 4 grams, Saturated Fat: 0.5 grams, Cholesterol: 5 milligrams, Sodium: 80 milligrams, Fiber: 4 grams, and Sugar: 18 grams.

BAKED OATMEAL WITH APPLES AND CINNAMON

- Total Time: 45 minutes
- Prep Time: 15 minutes
- Servings: 6

Ingredients:

- 2 cups old-fashioned rolled oats
- 1/2 cup chopped walnuts
- 1/4 cup brown sugar
- 1 teaspoon ground cinnamon
- 1/2 teaspoon ground nutmeg
- 1/4 teaspoon ground ginger
- 1/4 teaspoon salt
- 1 1/2 cups unsweetened almond milk
- 1 large egg
- 2 tablespoons maple syrup
- 1 teaspoon vanilla extract
- 2 medium apples, peeled, cored, and diced

Directions:

1. Prior to moving forward, it is of utmost importance to ensure that your oven has been preheated to 375°F (190°C) for optimal results. Additionally, grease an 8x8-inch baking dish with non-stick cooking spray or butter.
2. Start by mixing the dry ingredients in a large bowl. Combine the rolled oats, chopped walnuts, brown sugar, cinnamon, nutmeg, ginger, and salt. Give it a good stir to make sure everything is evenly distributed.
3. In another bowl, grab your wet ingredients: almond milk, egg, maple syrup, and vanilla extract. Whisk them together until well combined.
4. Add the diced apples to the dry oat mixture and stir to combine.
5. Pour the almond milk mixture over the oat and apple mixture, and stir gently until everything is well incorporated.
6. Transfer the baked oatmeal mixture to the prepared baking dish, spreading it evenly.
7. Bake for 30-35 minutes, or until the top is a beautiful golden brown and the center is firm to the touch.
8. Let the oatmeal cool slightly before serving. Take it out of the oven and wait 5-10 minutes for it to settle.
9. Serve the baked oatmeal warm, optionally with a drizzle of additional maple syrup, a sprinkle of cinnamon, or a scoop of Greek yogurt.

Nutritional breakdown per serving:

Calories: 250 kcal, Protein: 7 grams, Carbohydrates: 37 grams, Fat: 9 grams, Saturated Fat: 1 grams, Cholesterol: 35 milligrams, Sodium: 150 milligrams, Fiber: 5 grams, and Sugar: 15 grams.

POACHED EGGS ON SAUTÉED GREENS

- Total Time: 25 minutes
- Prep Time: 10 minutes
- Servings: 2

Ingredients:

- 4 large eggs
- 2 tablespoons white vinegar
- 2 cups chopped mixed greens (spinach, kale, chard)
- 1 tablespoon olive oil
- 2 cloves garlic, minced
- 1/4 teaspoon red pepper flakes (optional)
- 1/4 teaspoon salt
- 1/8 teaspoon ground black pepper

Directions:

1. Pour 3-4 inches of water into a medium saucepan and heat it on medium until it simmers gently. Add the white vinegar to the water.
2. Carefully crack the eggs, one at a time, into the simmering water. Poach the eggs for 4-5 minutes, or until the whites are completely set and the yolks are still runny.
3. Using a slotted spoon, gently transfer the poached eggs to a paper towel-lined plate.
4. Get olive oil hot in a large skillet over medium heat. Add the minced garlic and sauté for 1 minute, or until fragrant.
5. Add the chopped mixed greens to the skillet and sauté for 2-3 minutes, or until the greens are wilted and tender.
6. Season the sautéed greens with salt, black pepper, and red pepper flakes (if using). Stir to combine.
7. Divide the sautéed greens between two plates or bowls.
8. Carefully place the poached eggs on top of the sautéed greens.
9. Serve the poached eggs on sautéed greens immediately, while the eggs are still warm.

Nutritional breakdown per serving:

Calories: 210 kcal, Protein: 16 grams, Carbohydrates: 8 grams, Fat: 10 grams, Saturated Fat: 3 grams, Cholesterol: 372 milligrams, Sodium: 450 milligrams, Fiber: 3 grams, and Sugar: 1 grams.

GINGER AND TURMERIC OATMEAL

- Total Time: 25 minutes
- Prep Time: 10 minutes
- Servings: 4

Ingredients:

- 2 cups unsweetened almond milk
- 1 cup rolled oats
- 1 tablespoon freshly grated ginger
- 1 teaspoon ground turmeric
- 1/4 teaspoon ground cinnamon
- 1/4 teaspoon ground black pepper
- 2 tablespoons maple syrup
- 1/4 cup unsweetened shredded coconut
- 2 tablespoons chopped walnuts
- 1 tablespoon chia seeds

Directions:

1. Add almond milk, rolled oats, grated ginger, turmeric, cinnamon, and black pepper to a medium saucepan. Whisk well, then bring to a simmer over medium heat.
2. Lower the heat to low and simmer the oatmeal, stirring from time to time, for 12-15 minutes. The oatmeal is done when the oats are tender and the mixture reaches your preferred thickness.
3. Take the saucepan off the heat and stir in the maple syrup until incorporated.
4. Divide the ginger and turmeric oatmeal evenly among 4 serving bowls.
5. Top each serving with 1 tablespoon of unsweetened shredded coconut, 1/2 tablespoon of chopped walnuts, and 1/4 tablespoon of chia seeds.
6. Serve the oatmeal warm, and enjoy!

Nutritional breakdown per serving:

Calories: 250 kcal, Protein: 6 grams, Carbohydrates: 31 grams, Fat: 12 grams, Saturated Fat: 4 grams, Cholesterol: 0 milligrams, Sodium: 65 milligrams, Fiber: 6 grams, and Sugar: 9 grams.

VEGETABLE EGG MUFFINS

- Total Time: 40 minutes
- Prep Time: 15 minutes
- Servings: 12 muffins

Ingredients:

8 large eggs

- 1/2 cup unsweetened almond milk
- 1/4 cup grated Parmesan cheese
- 1/4 teaspoon salt
- 1/8 teaspoon ground black pepper
- 1 cup diced bell peppers (assorted colors)
- 1 cup diced spinach
- 1/2 cup diced onions
- 2 cloves garlic, minced
- 1 tablespoon fresh chopped herbs (basil, parsley, or chives)

Directions:

1. To commence with the recipe, start by preheating your oven to 375°F (190°C). Proceed with the preparation by greasing a 12-cup muffin tin using nonstick cooking spray or lining it with paper liners.
2. Whisk together the eggs, almond milk, Parmesan cheese, salt, and black pepper in a large bowl until well combined.
3. Incorporate the diced bell peppers, spinach, onions, minced garlic, and chopped fresh herbs into the pan, making sure to distribute them evenly.
4. Distribute the vegetable and egg mixture into the prepared muffin cups. Aim to fill each cup about three-quarters full.
5. Bake the egg muffins for 20-25 minutes, checking for doneness by inserting a toothpick in the center. Look for doneness by inserting a toothpick in the center. The muffins are finished when the toothpick comes out clean and the centers feel firm.
6. Take the muffin tin out of the oven and let the egg muffins cool in the pan for 5 minutes.
7. After allowing the egg muffins to cool for a bit, carefully transfer them to a wire rack. Let them cool completely for an additional 5 minutes before serving.

Nutritional breakdown per serving (1 muffin):

Calories: 90 kcal, Protein: 8 grams, Carbohydrates: 4 grams, Fat: 5 grams, Saturated Fat: 2 grams, Cholesterol: 125 milligrams, Sodium: 210 milligrams, Fiber: 1 grams, and Sugar: 1 grams.

NUT BUTTER AND BANANA TOAST

- Total Time: 10 minutes
- Prep Time: 5 minutes
- Servings: 2 slices of toast

Ingredients:

- 2 slices of whole-grain bread
- 2 tablespoons favorite nut butter (peanut, almond, cashew)
- 1 ripe banana, sliced
- 1 teaspoon of honey (optional)
- Cinnamon (for sprinkling, optional)

Directions:

1. Toast the two slices of whole-grain bread until they are lightly golden brown.
2. Spread 1 tablespoon of nut butter evenly over each slice of toast.
3. Arrange the sliced banana on top of the nut butter, covering the toast surface.
4. If desired, drizzle 1/2 teaspoon of honey over the banana slices on each slice of toast.
5. Sprinkle a pinch of cinnamon over the top of the banana slices (optional).
6. Serve the Nut Butter and Banana Toast immediately, while the toast is still warm.

Nutritional breakdown per serving:

Calories (1 slice of toast): 250 kcal, Protein: 8 grams, Carbohydrates: 27 grams, Fat: 14 grams, Saturated Fat: 2 grams, Cholesterol: 0 milligrams, Sodium: 200 milligrams, Fiber: 5 grams, and Sugar: 10 grams.

ZUCCHINI AND FETA FRITTERS

- Total Time: 30 minutes
- Prep Time: 15 minutes
- Servings: 8 fritters (4 servings)

Ingredients:

- 2 medium zucchini, grated (about 2 cups)
- 1/2 cup crumbled feta cheese
- 2 large eggs, beaten
- 1/4 cup all-purpose flour
- 2 tablespoons chopped fresh dill (or 1 teaspoon dried dill)
- 1 clove garlic, minced
- 1/4 teaspoon salt
- 1/8 teaspoon ground black pepper
- 2 tablespoons olive oil for cooking

Directions:

1. Press out excess moisture from the grated zucchini by squeezing it between paper towels or a clean kitchen towel.
2. In a medium bowl, combine grated zucchini, crumbled feta, beaten eggs, flour, chopped dill (fresh or dried), garlic, salt, and pepper. Mix well.
3. Get 1 tablespoon olive oil hot in a large non-stick skillet over medium heat.
4. Scoop heaping tablespoons of the zucchini mixture and gently place them in the hot skillet, flattening them slightly with the back of a spoon to form fritters.
5. Fry the fritters for 2-3 minutes per side, looking for a golden brown color. Be careful when flipping to maintain their shape.
6. Drain the cooked fritters on a plate lined with paper towels.
7. Use the rest of the zucchini mixture to make more fritters. Add a little more oil to the pan as needed to keep them from sticking.
8. Serve the Zucchini and Feta Fritters warm, garnished with additional chopped fresh dill, if desired.

Nutritional breakdown per serving (2 fritters):

Calories: 150 kcal, Protein: 7 grams, Carbohydrates: 9 grams, Fat: 10 grams, Saturated Fat: 4 grams, Cholesterol: 90 milligrams, Sodium: 310 milligrams, Fiber: 1 grams, and Sugar: 2 grams.

ANTI-INFLAMMATORY BREAKFAST BOWL WITH BEETS, CARROTS, AND AVOCADO

- Total Time: 25 minutes
- Prep Time: 15 minutes
- Servings: 1 bowl

Ingredients:

- 1 medium beet, peeled and grated (about 1/2 cup)
- 1 grated carrot (about 1/2 cup)
- 1/2 avocado, diced
- 1 tablespoon fresh lemon juice
- 1 tablespoon extra virgin olive oil
- 1 teaspoon ground turmeric
- 1/4 teaspoon ground ginger
- 1/4 teaspoon ground black pepper
- 1/8 teaspoon salt
- 2 eggs, cooked to your preference (e.g., poached, soft-boiled, or scrambled)
- 1 tablespoon chopped fresh parsley/cilantro (garnish)

Directions:

1. Toss together grated beet, carrot, and diced avocado in a medium bowl.
2. Start by mixing the dressing ingredients - lemon juice, olive oil, turmeric, ginger, black pepper, and salt - in a small bowl. Whisk the components together until they are well-combined.
3. Pour the dressing over the beet, carrot, and avocado mixture and gently toss to coat.
4. Cook the eggs according to your preferred method (poached, soft-boiled, or scrambled).
5. Transfer the beet, carrot, and avocado mixture to a serving bowl.
6. Top the mixture with the cooked eggs.
7. Garnish the bowl with the chopped fresh parsley or cilantro.
8. Serve immediately and enjoy.

Nutritional breakdown per serving:

Calories: 350 kcal, Protein: 12 grams, Carbohydrates: 25 grams, Fat: 25 grams, Saturated Fat: 5 grams, Cholesterol: 210 milligrams, Sodium: 300 milligrams, Fiber: 9 grams, and Sugar: 11 grams.

MATCHA GREEN TEA LATTE

- Total Time: 10 minutes
- Prep Time: 5 minutes
- Servings: 1 latte

Ingredients:

- 1 teaspoon matcha green tea powder
- 2 tablespoons hot water (just off the boil)
- 1 cup unsweetened almond milk (or milk of your choice)
- 1-2 teaspoons maple syrup or honey (optional, to taste)
- Pinch of ground cinnamon (for garnish)

Directions:

1. In a small container, combine the matcha green tea powder and hot water. Whisk the components together until a uniform, smooth paste is formed, free of any lumps.
2. Set a small saucepan over medium heat and warm the almond milk, stirring it occasionally, until it becomes hot and steaming, but be careful not to let it reach a boiling temperature.
3. Remove the saucepan from the heat and use a milk frother or small whisk to froth and foam the almond milk.
4. Carefully pour the frothed almond milk into the bowl or cup with the matcha paste, and whisk or stir to combine.
5. If desired, stir in 1-2 teaspoons of maple syrup or honey to sweeten the latte to your taste.
6. Pour the matcha latte into a serving mug or glass.
7. Garnish the top of the latte with a light dusting of ground cinnamon.
8. Serve immediately and enjoy your Matcha Green Tea Latte!

Nutritional breakdown per serving:

Calories: 80 kcal, Protein: 3 grams, Carbohydrates: 9 grams, Fat: 3 grams, Saturated Fat: 0 grams, Cholesterol: 0 milligrams, Sodium: 75 milligrams, Fiber: 2 grams, and Sugar: 3 grams.

VEGGIE-PACKED BREAKFAST BURRITO

- Total Time: 30 minutes
- Prep Time: 20 minutes
- Servings: 4 burritos

Ingredients:

- 4 large whole wheat tortillas
- 4 eggs, scrambled
- 1 cup diced bell peppers (mix of red, yellow, and/or orange)
- 1/2 cup diced onion
- 1 cup chopped spinach or kale
- 1/2 cup diced tomatoes
- 1/2 avocado, diced
- 2 tablespoons crumbled feta cheese (optional)
- 2 tablespoons salsa (optional)
- 1 tablespoon olive oil
- 1/4 teaspoon salt
- 1/4 teaspoon ground black pepper

Directions:

1. Place a large non-stick skillet on the stovetop and set the heat to medium. Then, pour in the olive oil.
2. Next, add the diced bell peppers and onion to the heated skillet. Sauté for 5-7 minutes, or until the vegetables are tender and starting to caramelize.
3. Toss the chopped spinach or kale into the skillet and let it cook for 2-3 minutes, until the greens have wilted down.
4. In a separate bowl, whisk the eggs and season with salt and pepper.
5. Pour the eggs into the skillet with the sautéed vegetables. Gently stir and scramble the eggs until they are fully cooked, about 3-5 minutes.
6. Take the skillet off the heat and then stir in the diced tomatoes.
7. Warm the whole wheat tortillas according to the package instructions.
8. Divide the egg and vegetable mixture evenly among the 4 tortillas.
9. Top each burrito with diced avocado and crumbled feta cheese (if using).
10. If desired, add a spoonful of salsa to each burrito.
11. Begin by folding the bottom of the tortilla upwards. Take the tortilla and fold the sides inwards. Finally, keep rolling the tortilla tightly to create a compact burrito shape.
12. Serve the veggie-packed breakfast burritos immediately.

Nutritional breakdown per serving:

Calories: 350 kcal, Protein: 16 grams, Carbohydrates: 35 grams, Fat: 18 grams, Saturated Fat: 4 grams, Cholesterol: 200 milligrams, Sodium: 660 milligrams, Fiber: 7 grams, and Sugar: 4 grams.

BLUEBERRY AND ALMOND CHIA PUDDING

- Total Time: 4 hours (includes chilling time)
- Prep Time: 15 minutes
- Servings: 4

Ingredients:

- 1/4 cup chia seeds
- 1 1/2 cups unsweetened almond milk
- 2 tablespoons maple syrup
- 1 teaspoon vanilla extract
- 1/4 teaspoon ground cinnamon
- 1 cup fresh or frozen blueberries
- 2 tablespoons slivered almonds

Directions:

1. Measure out the chia seeds, almond milk, maple syrup, vanilla extract, and ground cinnamon, and add them to a medium-sized mixing bowl. Then, use a whisk to thoroughly combine all the ingredients until they are fully incorporated and the mixture has a smooth, uniform consistency.
2. Cover the bowl containing the chia seed mixture and refrigerate it for at least 4 hours, or overnight, stirring the contents occasionally. Refrigerating the mixture will cause it to thicken and take on a pudding-like consistency.
3. In a separate bowl, gently toss the blueberries to coat them.
4. To serve, divide the chia pudding mixture evenly among 4 serving bowls or jars.
5. Top each portion of chia pudding with a portion of the blueberries.
6. Sprinkle the slivered almonds over the top of the blueberries.
7. Serve chilled and enjoy your Blueberry and Almond Chia Pudding!

Nutritional breakdown per serving:

Calories: 190 kcal, Protein: 5 grams, Carbohydrates: 24 grams, Fat: 9 grams, Saturated Fat: 1 grams, Cholesterol: 0 milligrams, Sodium: 45 milligrams, Fiber: 7 grams, and Sugar: 12 grams.

SAUTÉED MUSHROOMS AND ASPARAGUS ON WHOLE GRAIN TOAST

- Total Time: 25 minutes
- Prep Time: 15 minutes
- Servings: 4

Ingredients:

- 8 ounces mixed mushrooms (such as cremini, shiitake, and oyster), sliced
- 1 bunch asparagus, trimmed & cut into 1-inch pieces
- 2 tablespoons olive oil
- 2 cloves garlic, minced
- 1/4 teaspoon red pepper flakes (optional)
- 1/4 cup vegetable broth
- 2 tablespoons chopped fresh parsley
- 1/4 teaspoon salt
- 1/4 teaspoon ground black pepper
- 4 slices whole grain bread, toasted

Directions:

1. Bring olive oil to a simmer in a large skillet over medium-high heat.
2. Sauté the sliced mushrooms in the skillet for 5-7 minutes, until they're lightly browned and release their moisture.
3. Add the chopped asparagus, garlic, and red pepper flakes (if using) to the skillet. Sauté for an additional 3-5 minutes, or until the asparagus is tender-crisp.
4. Next, pour the vegetable broth into the skillet and use a utensil to stir and scrape up any flavorful browned bits that have formed on the bottom of the pan.
5. Allow the mixture to simmer for 2-3 minutes, or until the broth has reduced slightly and the vegetables are coated in a light sauce.
6. Take the skillet off the heat and then stir in the chopped parsley, salt, and black pepper.
7. Toast the whole grain bread slices until lightly golden brown.
8. Divide the sautéed mushroom and asparagus mixture evenly among the 4 toast slices.
9. Serve the Sautéed Mushrooms and Asparagus on Whole Grain Toast immediately, while the toast is still warm.

Nutritional breakdown per serving:

Calories (1 slice of toast with vegetable topping): 205 kcal, Protein: 8 grams, Carbohydrates: 21 grams, Fat: 10 grams, Saturated Fat: 1.5 grams, Cholesterol: 0 milligrams, Sodium: 340 milligrams, Fiber: 5 grams, and Sugar: 2 grams.

COCONUT CHIA SEED PUDDING WITH MANGO

- Total Time: 6 hours (includes chilling time)
- Prep Time: 20 minutes
- Servings: 4

Ingredients:

- 1/2 cup chia seeds
- 1 cup unsweetened coconut milk
- 1/2 cup unsweetened almond milk
- 2 tablespoons maple syrup
- 1 teaspoon vanilla extract
- 1/4 teaspoon ground cinnamon
- 1 ripe mango, diced
- 2 tablespoons toasted coconut flakes

Directions:

1. In a medium bowl, whisk together the chia seeds, coconut milk, almond milk, maple syrup, vanilla extract, and ground cinnamon until well combined.
2. Place a cover over the bowl containing the chia seed mixture. Then, refrigerate the mixture for at least 4 hours, or up to 24 hours, stirring it occasionally. Refrigerating the chia seed mixture will cause it to thicken to a pudding-like consistency.
3. When ready to serve, divide the coconut chia seed pudding evenly among 4 serving bowls or jars.
4. Top each portion of chia seed pudding with a generous amount of diced mango.
5. Top the mango with a sprinkling of toasted coconut flakes.
6. Serve chilled and enjoy your Coconut Chia Seed Pudding with Mango!

Nutritional breakdown per serving:

Calories: 250 kcal, Protein: 6 grams, Carbohydrates: 26 grams, Fat: 14 grams, Saturated Fat: 8 grams, Cholesterol: 0 milligrams, Sodium: 55 milligrams, Fiber: 8 grams, and Sugar: 11 grams.

SPINACH AND TOMATO OMELET

- Total Time: 20 minutes
- Prep Time: 10 minutes
- Servings: 1

Ingredients:

- 2 large eggs
- 1 tablespoon milk
- 1/4 teaspoon salt
- 1/8 teaspoon ground black pepper
- 1 teaspoon olive oil
- 1 cup fresh baby spinach, roughly chopped
- 1/4 cup diced tomatoes
- 1 tablespoon grated cheddar cheese

Directions:

1. Grab a small bowl and whisk your eggs, milk, salt, and pepper until everything is smooth and incorporated.
2. Start by preheating a small non-stick skillet over medium heat. Once hot, swirl in some olive oil to coat the bottom of the pan.
3. Gently pour the egg mixture into the preheated skillet. Let it cook undisturbed for 20-30 seconds, allowing the bottom to set.
4. Use your spatula to gently nudge the cooked egg towards the center of the pan. As you do this, tilt the skillet slightly. This lets the uncooked egg from the edges flow towards the bottom to cook.
5. Once the bottom is set but the top is still slightly runny, sprinkle the chopped spinach and diced tomatoes over one half of the omelet.
6. Fold the other half of the omelet over the spinach and tomato filling.
7. For a dramatic reveal, carefully slide the folded omelet onto a waiting plate. Then, shower it with a generous sprinkle of grated cheddar cheese.
8. Serve the Spinach and Tomato Omelet immediately, while hot.

Nutritional breakdown per serving:

Calories: 290 kcal, Protein: 22 grams, Carbohydrates: 8 grams, Fat: 19 grams, Saturated Fat: 6 grams, Cholesterol: 372 milligrams, Sodium: 600 milligrams, Fiber: 2 grams, and Sugar: 3 grams.

GINGER PEACH SMOOTHIE

- Total Time: 10 minutes
- Prep Time: 10 minutes
- Servings: 2

Ingredients:

- 2 ripe peaches, pitted and chopped
- 1 cup unsweetened almond milk
- 1/2 cup plain Greek yogurt
- 2 tablespoons honey
- 1 tablespoon freshly grated ginger
- 1/2 teaspoon ground cinnamon
- 1/4 teaspoon ground nutmeg
- 1 cup crushed ice

Directions:

1. In a high-speed blender, combine the chopped peaches, almond milk, Greek yogurt, honey, grated ginger, cinnamon, and nutmeg.
2. Achieve smoothie perfection! Toss the crushed ice into your blender. Next, hit high speed and blend for 1-2 minutes, until you have a luxuriously smooth and creamy beverage.
3. Taste and adjust sweetness or ginger flavor as needed.
4. Pour the Ginger Peach Smoothie into two glasses and serve immediately.

Nutritional breakdown per serving:

Calories: 180 kcal, Protein: 8 grams, Carbohydrates: 34 grams, Fat: 3 grams, Saturated Fat: 1 grams, Cholesterol: 10 milligrams, Sodium: 45 milligrams, Fiber: 3 grams, and Sugar: 28 grams.

ROASTED SWEET POTATO AND KALE HASH

- Total Time: 40 minutes
- Prep Time: 15 minutes
- Servings: 4

Ingredients:

- 2 sweet potatoes, peeled & diced (1/2 inch cubes)
- 2 tablespoons olive oil, divided
- 1 teaspoon smoked paprika
- 1/2 teaspoon garlic powder
- 1/2 teaspoon salt
- 1/4 teaspoon black pepper
- 1 bunch kale, chopped (discard stems)
- 1 red onion, diced
- 2 cloves garlic, minced
- 1 tablespoon apple cider vinegar
- 2 eggs, cooked to desired doneness (optional)

Directions:

1. Before you start preparing the recipe, it is advised to preheat your oven to 400°F (200°C) to ensure that the cooking conditions are optimal.
2. Combine diced sweet potatoes in a large bowl with olive oil, smoked paprika, garlic powder, a sprinkle of salt, and some black pepper.
3. Evenly distribute the seasoned sweet potato cubes on a parchment-lined baking sheet.
4. Roast the sweet potatoes for 20-25 minutes, giving them a flip halfway through. Aim for tender and golden brown on all sides.
5. With the sweet potatoes baking in the oven, take advantage of that time by preheating 1 tablespoon of olive oil in a large skillet over medium heat.
6. Place the chopped kale into the preheated skillet and sauté it for 2-3 minutes, allowing the kale to wilt and become tender.
7. Toss in the diced red onion and minced garlic. Sauté for 3-4 more minutes, until the onions are softened.
8. Incorporate the roasted sweet potato cubes and apple cider vinegar into the skillet. Simmer for 2-3 minutes, letting the flavors meld together.
9. Give the sweet potatoes a taste test. If you think they need a flavor kick, add a sprinkle of salt and pepper.
10. Serve the Roasted Sweet Potato and Kale Hash warm, optionally topped with a fried or poached egg.

Nutritional breakdown per serving:

Calories: 220 kcal, Protein: 5 grams, Carbohydrates: 33 grams, Fat: 8 grams, Saturated Fat: 1 grams, Cholesterol: 0 milligrams, Sodium: 360 milligrams, Fiber: 6 grams, and Sugar: 9 grams.

BUCKWHEAT GROATS WITH BERRIES AND ALMONDS

- Total Time: 25 minutes
- Prep Time: 10 minutes
- Servings: 4

Ingredients:

- 1 cup raw buckwheat groats
- 2 cups unsweetened almond milk
- 1/4 teaspoon salt
- 1 cup mixed berries (blueberries, raspberries, blackberries)
- 1/4 cup raw sliced almonds
- 2 tablespoons pure maple syrup
- 1 teaspoon ground cinnamon
- 1/4 teaspoon ground nutmeg

Directions:

1. In a medium saucepan, combine the buckwheat groats, almond milk, and salt. Bring on the bubbles! Heat the mixture to a rapid boil over high heat.
2. Let the mixture boil vigorously for a minute, then reduce heat to low. Simmer for 12-15 minutes, covered, to allow the flavors to meld. You'll know it's done when the buckwheat groats are tender and most of the liquid has been absorbed.
3. Remove the saucepan from the heat and let the buckwheat groats sit, covered, for an additional 5 minutes.
4. Fluff the cooked buckwheat groats with a fork, and then stir in the fresh mixed berries, sliced almonds, maple syrup, cinnamon, and nutmeg until well combined.
5. Enjoy your Buckwheat Groats with Berries and Almonds! Serve them warm for a comforting breakfast, or chill them in the fridge for a refreshing treat later.

Nutritional breakdown per serving:

Calories: 270 kcal, Protein: 7 grams, Carbohydrates: 41 grams, Fat: 10 grams, Saturated Fat: 1 grams, Cholesterol: 0 milligrams, Sodium: 150 milligrams, Fiber: 7 grams, and Sugar: 12 grams.

SAUTÉED GREENS WITH POACHED EGG AND AVOCADO

- Total Time: 30 minutes
- Prep Time: 15 minutes
- Servings: 4

Ingredients:

- 1 bunch kale, chopped (discard stems)
- 1 bunch fresh Swiss chard, stems removed and leaves chopped
- 2 tablespoons extra-virgin olive oil
- 3 cloves garlic, minced
- 1/4 teaspoon red pepper flakes (optional)
- 1/4 cup vegetable or chicken broth
- 1 tablespoon lemon juice
- 1/2 teaspoon salt
- 1/4 teaspoon black pepper
- 4 large eggs
- 2 ripe avocados, sliced
- 2 tablespoons toasted pumpkin seeds (optional)

Directions:

1. Heat olive oil (large skillet/Dutch oven, medium heat). Sauté minced garlic (add red pepper flakes for heat, optional). Sauté for 1 minute, until fragrant.
2. Toss in the chopped kale and Swiss chard. Sauté for 3-5 minutes, giving them a stir now and then, until they become soft and wilted.
3. Deglaze the pan with vegetable or chicken broth and a squeeze of lemon juice. Season with salt and black pepper. Continue to cook the greens for an additional 2-3 minutes, allowing the liquid to slightly evaporate and the flavors to meld.
4. While the greens are cooking, bring a large pot of water to a gentle simmer. Crack the eggs one at a time and gently slip them into the simmering water. Poach the eggs gently for 4-6 minutes. Watch for firm whites and yolks cooked to your preference.
5. Using a slotted spoon, carefully transfer the poached eggs to a paper towel-lined plate.
6. To serve, divide the sautéed greens among 4 plates. For the perfect finishing touch, add a poached egg and sliced avocado to each serving. Sprinkle with toasted pumpkin seeds, if desired.

Nutritional breakdown per serving:

Calories: 360 kcal, Protein: 16 grams, Carbohydrates: 23 grams, Fat: 24 grams, Saturated Fat: 4 grams, Cholesterol: 186 milligrams, Sodium: 509 milligrams, Fiber: 11 grams, and Sugar: 2 grams.

ANTI-INFLAMMATORY BREAKFAST BOWL WITH TURMERIC-ROASTED CAULIFLOWER

- Total Time: 45 minutes
- Prep Time: 20 minutes
- Servings: 4

Ingredients:

- 1 head of cauliflower, cut into florets
- 2 tablespoons extra-virgin olive oil
- 1 teaspoon ground turmeric
- 1/2 teaspoon ground cumin
- 1/4 teaspoon ground cinnamon
- 1/4 teaspoon salt
- 1/4 teaspoon black pepper
- 4 large eggs
- 1 avocado, sliced
- 1 cup cooked quinoa
- 1/2 cup sliced cucumber
- 2 tablespoons toasted pumpkin seeds
- 2 tablespoons fresh parsley, chopped
- 1 tablespoon lemon juice

Dressing:

- 1/4 cup extra-virgin olive oil
- 2 tablespoons apple cider vinegar
- 1 tablespoon honey
- 1 teaspoon Dijon mustard
- 1/4 teaspoon salt
- 1/8 teaspoon black pepper

Directions:

1. Before you start preparing the recipe, it is advised to preheat your oven to 400°F (200°C) to ensure that the cooking conditions are optimal.
2. In a large bowl, toss the florets with 2 tablespoons olive oil, turmeric, cumin, cinnamon, salt, and pepper to evenly coat them.

3. Arrange the seasoned cauliflower florets on a baking sheet for roasting. Place the cauliflower florets in the preheated oven for 20-25 minutes, until they reach a tender texture with a light golden brown color.
4. While the dish is in the oven, take the opportunity to make the dressing. In a small mixing bowl, whisk together all the dressing ingredients until they are fully incorporated.
5. Start by bringing some water to a gentle simmer in a saucepan. One at a time, crack the eggs and carefully slip them into the simmering water. Allow the eggs to poach for 4-6 minutes, until the whites are fully set and the yolks have reached your preferred level of doneness.
6. Using a slotted spoon, carefully transfer the poached eggs to a paper towel-lined plate.
7. To assemble the breakfast bowls, divide the cooked quinoa among 4 serving bowls. Top each bowl with the roasted turmeric cauliflower, sliced avocado, sliced cucumber, and a poached egg.
8. Drizzle the dressing over the bowls and garnish with the toasted pumpkin seeds and chopped parsley.
9. Serve the Anti-Inflammatory Breakfast Bowl with Turmeric-Roasted Cauliflower immediately.

Nutritional breakdown per serving:

Calories: 410 kcal, Protein: 13 grams, Carbohydrates: 33 grams, Fat: 27 grams, Saturated Fat: 4 grams, Cholesterol: 186 milligrams, Sodium: 416 milligrams, Fiber: 9 grams, and Sugar: 8 grams.

NUT AND SEED GRANOLA WITH GREEK YOGURT

- Total Time: 45 minutes
- Prep Time: 15 minutes
- Servings: 6

Ingredients:

Granola:

- 2 cups rolled oats
- 1 cup raw almonds, coarsely chopped
- 1/2 cup raw pecans, coarsely chopped
- 1/2 cup raw pumpkin seeds
- 1/2 cup raw sunflower seeds
- 1/4 cup pure maple syrup
- 2 tablespoons coconut oil, melted
- 1 teaspoon ground cinnamon
- 1/4 teaspoon ground ginger
- 1/4 teaspoon sea salt
- Yogurt Parfait:
- 2 cups plain Greek yogurt
- 1 cup fresh berries
- 2 tablespoons honey

Directions:

Granola:

1. Before you start preparing the recipe, it is advised to preheat your oven to 325°F (165°C) to ensure that the cooking conditions are optimal. Prep your baking sheet for effortless baking by lining it with parchment paper.
2. Toss rolled oats, chopped almonds, pecans, pumpkin seeds, and sunflower seeds together in a large bowl.
3. In a small bowl, whisk together the maple syrup, melted coconut oil, cinnamon, ginger, and sea salt.
4. Drizzle the maple syrup mixture in a thin, even layer over the oat and nut mixture. Using a large spoon, give it a good stir to ensure everything is beautifully coated.
5. Spread the granola mixture evenly across the prepared baking sheet.
6. Bake for 20-25 minutes, stirring occasionally for a beautiful golden brown color and a delightful nutty aroma.

7. Take the granola out of the oven and transfer it to the baking sheet to cool completely.
8. Grab a medium bowl and gently fold in honey to the Greek yogurt until everything is well incorporated.
9. In six serving glasses or bowls, layer the granola, yogurt mixture, and fresh berries, repeating the layers until all the ingredients are used up.
10. Serve the Nut and Seed Granola with Greek Yogurt parfaits immediately.

Nutritional breakdown per serving:

Calories: 395 kcal, Protein: 16 grams, Carbohydrates: 38 grams, Fat: 21 grams, Saturated Fat: 6 grams, Cholesterol: 20 milligrams, Sodium: 115 milligrams, Fiber: 6 grams, and Sugar: 16 grams.

BAKED SALMON AND ASPARAGUS FRITTATA

- Total Time: 50 minutes
- Prep Time: 15 minutes
- Servings: 6

Ingredients:

- 8 large eggs
- 1/2 cup unsweetened almond milk
- 2 tablespoons fresh dill, chopped
- 1 teaspoon Dijon mustard
- 1/2 teaspoon sea salt
- 1/4 teaspoon ground black pepper
- 1 tablespoon olive oil
- 1 pound asparagus, trimmed & cut into 1-in pieces (or spears)
- 8 ounces cooked salmon, flaked
- 1/2 cup crumbled feta cheese

Directions:

1. Before you continue, make sure that your oven is preheated to 375°F (190°C). Grease a 9-inch pie dish or oven-safe skillet with nonstick cooking spray.
2. In a large bowl, whisk together the eggs, almond milk, fresh dill, Dijon mustard, sea salt, and ground black pepper until well combined.
3. Pour a bit of olive oil into a large skillet and place it over medium heat to preheat. Add the asparagus and give them a good sauté for 3-5 minutes. You want them tender-crisp when they're done.
4. Spread the sautéed asparagus evenly in the prepared pie dish or skillet. Top with the flaked salmon.
5. Gently pour the egg mixture over the salmon and asparagus, distributing the ingredients evenly.
6. Top the frittata with a sprinkle of crumbled feta cheese.
7. Bake the frittata for 30-35 minutes, or until the center is set and the top is golden brown.
8. Once the frittata is finished baking, take it out of the oven and allow it to cool for 5 minutes before slicing and serving.

Nutritional breakdown per serving:

Calories: 254 kcal, Protein: 24 grams, Carbohydrates: 6 grams, Fat: 15 grams, Saturated Fat: 4 grams, Cholesterol: 251 milligrams, Sodium: 538 milligrams, Fiber: 2 grams, and Sugar: 2 grams.

GINGER LEMON TEA

- Total Brewing Time: 20 minutes
- Prep Time: 5 minutes
- Servings: 4

Ingredients:

- 4 cups water
- 2 fresh ginger, peeled & thinly sliced
- 2 tablespoons honey
- 1/4 cup fresh lemon juice (2 med. lemons)
- 1 lemon, thinly sliced for garnish (optional)

Directions:

1. First, bring the water in a medium saucepan to a rolling boil over high heat.
2. Once the water is boiling, reduce the heat to medium-low and add the sliced fresh ginger.
3. Simmer the ginger in the water for 15-20 minutes, allowing the ginger to infuse the water and create a strong ginger flavor.
4. Take the saucepan off the heat and stir in the honey until it disappears completely.
5. Pour the tea through a fine-mesh sieve to get rid of the ginger slices.
6. Stir in the freshly squeezed lemon juice.
7. Serve the Ginger Lemon Tea hot, garnished with thin lemon slices, if desired.

Nutritional breakdown per serving:

Calories: 50 kcal, Protein: 0 grams, Carbohydrates: 13 grams, Fat: 0 grams, Saturated Fat: 0 grams, Cholesterol: 0 milligrams, Sodium: 5 milligrams, Fiber: 0 grams, and Sugar: 11 grams.

AVOCADO AND TOMATO TOAST WITH MICROGREENS

- Total Time: 15 minutes
- Prep Time: 10 minutes
- Servings: 2

Ingredients:

- 2 slices whole-grain or sourdough bread
- 1 ripe avocado, pitted and mashed
- 1 cup cherry tomatoes, halved
- 2 tablespoons crumbled feta cheese
- 1/4 cup microgreens (such as sunflower, radish, or arugula microgreens)
- 1 tablespoon extra-virgin olive oil
- 1 tablespoon balsamic glaze
- 1/4 teaspoon sea salt
- 1/8 teaspoon ground black pepper

Directions:

1. Toast the two pieces of bread until they reach a beautiful golden brown color.
2. Mash the avocado in a small bowl with a fork until it reaches a smooth, spreadable texture.
3. Spread the mashed avocado evenly over the toasted bread slices.
4. Top the avocado toast with the halved cherry tomatoes, evenly distributing them across the surface.
5. Crumble feta cheese over the tomatoes for a delightful salty touch.
6. In a small bowl, gently toss the microgreens with the extra-virgin olive oil.
7. Arrange the dressed microgreens on top of the feta cheese.
8. Drizzle the balsamic glaze over the entire toast.
9. To finish, season the dish with a light sprinkling of sea salt and a liberal grinding of fresh black pepper.
10. Serve immediately and enjoy.

Nutritional breakdown per serving:

Calories: 291 kcal, Protein: 8 grams, Carbohydrates: 27 grams, Fat: 18 grams, Saturated Fat: 4 grams, Cholesterol: 15 milligrams, Sodium: 436 milligrams, Fiber: 8 grams, and Sugar: 4 grams.

BAKED OATMEAL CUPS WITH BERRIES AND NUTS

- Total Time: 40 minutes
- Prep Time: 15 minutes
- Servings: 12 cups

Ingredients:

- 2 cups old-fashioned rolled oats
- 1/2 cup chopped walnuts or pecans
- 1/4 cup brown sugar
- 1 teaspoon baking powder
- 1/2 teaspoon ground cinnamon
- 1/4 teaspoon salt
- 1 cup unsweetened almond milk
- 1 large egg
- 2 tbsp melted coconut oil (or butter)
- 1 teaspoon vanilla extract
- 1 cup mixed berries (blueberries, raspberries, blackberries)

Directions:

1. Before you continue, make sure that your oven is preheated to 375°F (190°C) for optimal results. Additionally, grease a 12-cup muffin tin or line it with paper liners.
2. In a large bowl, toss together rolled oats, chopped nuts, brown sugar, baking powder, cinnamon, and a pinch of salt. Give it a good stir to make sure everything is evenly distributed.
3. In another bowl, combine almond milk, egg, melted coconut oil, and vanilla extract. Give it a good whisk until everything is incorporated and there are no streaks.
4. Grab a new bowl and whisk together the almond milk, egg, melted coconut oil (butter works too!), and vanilla extract. Make sure it's all nicely combined.
5. Gently fold in the mixed berries, reserving a few for the top of the cups.
6. Scoop the oatmeal mixture evenly into the prepared muffin cups, filling them about 3/4 full.
7. Top each cup with a few additional berries.
8. Bake for 20-25 minutes, or until the oatmeal cups are golden brown and set.
9. Let the oatmeal cups settle in the muffin tin for 5 minutes after baking. The last step: transfer the oatmeal cups to a wire rack to cool down completely.
10. Present the dish either warm or at room temperature, and then enjoy!

Nutritional breakdown per serving:

Calories (1 cup): 165 kcal, Protein: 4 grams, Carbohydrates: 19 grams, Fat: 9 grams, Saturated Fat: 4 grams, Cholesterol: 16 milligrams, Sodium: 126 milligrams, Fiber: 3 grams, and Sugar: 8 grams.

VEGGIE-PACKED BREAKFAST CASSEROLE

- Total Time: 1 hour 15 minutes
- Prep Time: 30 minutes
- Servings: 8

Ingredients:

8 large eggs

- 1 cup unsweetened almond milk
- 1/4 cup grated Parmesan cheese
- 1 teaspoon dried oregano
- 1/2 teaspoon garlic powder
- 1/4 teaspoon red pepper flakes (optional)
- 1/4 teaspoon salt
- 1/8 teaspoon ground black pepper
- 2 tablespoons olive oil
- 1 cup diced bell peppers
- 1 cup diced zucchini
- 1 cup diced mushrooms
- 1 cup diced onion
- 2 cups baby spinach leaves
- 1 cup cherry tomatoes, halved

Directions:

1. To begin, make sure to preheat your oven to 375°F (190°C) before starting to cook, as this will help ensure the best possible results. After that, make sure to grease a 9x13-inch baking dish.
2. In a large bowl, whisk together the eggs, almond milk, Parmesan cheese, oregano, garlic powder, red pepper flakes (if using), salt, and black pepper until well combined.
3. Heat a large skillet over medium heat. Add olive oil and diced bell peppers, zucchini, mushrooms, and onion. Sauté 5-7 minutes until tender-crisp.
4. Add the sautéed vegetables and the baby spinach leaves to the egg mixture. Stir gently to combine.
5. Pour the egg-vegetable mixture into the prepared baking dish, spreading it out evenly.
6. Scatter the halved cherry tomatoes across the surface of the casserole, distributing them evenly.

7. Place the casserole in the oven and bake it for 35-40 minutes, or until the center is set and the top has a lightly golden hue.
8. Take the casserole out of the oven and let it sit for 5-10 minutes before serving.
9. Cut the casserole into 8 equal portions and serve warm.

Nutritional breakdown per serving:

Calories: 180 kcal, Protein: 12 grams, Carbohydrates: 9 grams, Fat: 11 grams, Saturated Fat: 1 grams, Cholesterol: 195 milligrams, Sodium: 340 milligrams, Fiber: 2 grams, and Sugar: 4 grams.

CHAPTER 2
LUNCH RECIPES

CRUNCHY QUINOA, TENDER KALE, AND ROASTED BEET SALAD WITH CREAMY GOAT CHEESE

- Total Time: 1 hour 15 minutes
- Prep Time: 30 minutes
- Servings: 4

Ingredients:

- 3 medium-sized beets, peeled and cut into 1-inch cubes
- 2 tablespoons olive oil, divided
- 1/2 teaspoon salt, divided
- 1/4 teaspoon ground black pepper, divided
- 1 cup uncooked quinoa, rinsed
- 2 cups vegetable or chicken broth
- 4 cups chopped kale, stems removed
- 1/4 cup crumbled goat cheese
- 2 tablespoons toasted walnuts or pecans
- 2 tablespoons balsamic vinegar
- 1 tablespoon Dijon mustard
- 1 tablespoon honey
- 1 clove garlic, minced

Directions:

1. Get the oven going first - preheat it to 400°F (200°C). Next up, prep the baking sheet for easy cleanup - line it with parchment paper.
2. Get the beets ready for roasting! In a medium bowl, toss the cubed beets with 1 tablespoon olive oil, 1/4 teaspoon salt, and 1/8 teaspoon black pepper. Once the baking sheet is prepped, evenly spread the beets for roasting. Aim for 25-30 minutes, or until tender and lightly caramelized. Let them cool before continuing.
3. At the stove, use a medium saucepan to combine the quinoa and broth. Simmer for 15-20 minutes, covered, until the quinoa is tender and absorbs all the liquid. After cooking, fluff quinoa with a fork and cool slightly for use.
4. In a large bowl, toss together the chopped kale, roasted beets, cooked quinoa, crumbled goat cheese, and toasted walnuts or pecans.
5. In a small bowl, mix together the remaining 1 tablespoon olive oil, ¼ teaspoon salt, and ⅛ teaspoon black pepper. Whisk in balsamic vinegar, Dijon mustard, honey, and minced garlic until well combined.

6. Dress the kale and quinoa salad with the prepared dressing. Gently toss everything until the salad is evenly coated.
7. Serve the Kale and Quinoa Salad with Roasted Beets and Goat Cheese at room temperature or chilled.

Nutritional breakdown per serving:

Calories: 310 kcal, Protein: 10 grams, Carbohydrates: 35 grams, Fat: 15 grams, Saturated Fat: 4 grams, Cholesterol: 10 milligrams, Sodium: 590 milligrams, Fiber: 6 grams, and Sugar: 10 grams.

GRILLED CHICKEN AND MANGO SALAD WITH AVOCADO AND LIME DRESSING

- Total Time: 35 minutes
- Prep Time: 20 minutes
- Servings: 4

Ingredients:

- 4 chicken breasts (or 1.5 lbs chicken breasts for a more precise amount)
- 2 tablespoons olive oil, divided
- 1 teaspoon chili powder
- 1/2 teaspoon salt
- 1/4 teaspoon ground black pepper
- 1 ripe avocado, pitted and diced
- 2 mangoes, peeled and diced
- 1 red bell pepper, diced
- 4 cups mixed greens
- 1/4 cup crumbled feta cheese
- 2 tablespoons chopped fresh cilantro

Dressing:

- 1 ripe avocado, pitted and mashed
- 2 tablespoons fresh lime juice
- 1 tablespoon honey
- 1 tablespoon olive oil
- 1 clove garlic, minced
- 1/4 teaspoon salt
- 1/8 teaspoon ground black pepper

Directions:

1. Fire up your grill or grill pan for medium-high heat.
2. For a flavorful kick, create a simple spice rub in a small bowl. Combine 1 tablespoon olive oil, chili powder, ½ teaspoon salt, and ¼ teaspoon black pepper. Rub the mixture over the chicken breasts.
3. Grill the chicken for 5-7 minutes per side, or until it's cooked through and reaches an internal temperature of 165°F (75°C). Take the chicken off the grill and let it rest for 5 minutes. Break down the chicken into bite-sized pieces by slicing or chopping.

4. To make the dressing, whisk together the following ingredients in a medium bowl: mashed avocado, lime juice, honey, olive oil, minced garlic, salt, and black pepper.
5. Build your salad in a large bowl by adding mixed greens, grilled chicken, diced mango, red bell pepper, avocado, crumbled feta cheese, and chopped fresh cilantro.
6. Drizzle the avocado-lime dressing over the salad and toss gently to coat the ingredients evenly.
7. Serve the Grilled Chicken and Mango Salad immediately.

Nutritional breakdown per serving:

Calories: 400 kcal, Protein: 32 grams, Carbohydrates: 29 grams, Fat: 21 grams, Saturated Fat: 5 grams, Cholesterol: 80 milligrams, Sodium: 550 milligrams, Fiber: 7 grams, and Sugar: 16 grams.

VEGETABLE CURRY WITH CHICKPEAS AND BASMATI RICE

- Total Time: 45 minutes
- Prep Time: 20 minutes
- Servings: 4

Ingredients:

Curry:

- 2 tablespoons coconut oil
- 1 large onion, diced
- 3 cloves garlic, minced
- 1 tablespoon grated fresh ginger
- 2 teaspoons garam masala
- 1 teaspoon ground cumin
- 1 teaspoon ground coriander
- 1/2 teaspoon ground turmeric
- 1/4 teaspoon cayenne pepper
- 1 cup diced tomatoes (fresh or canned)
- 1 cup vegetable broth
- 1 (15-ounce) can chickpeas, rinsed and drained
- 1 medium cauliflower, cut into florets
- 1 medium sweet potato, peeled and diced
- 1 cup frozen peas
- 1/4 cup chopped fresh cilantro
- Salt and black pepper to taste

Rice:

- 1 cup basmati rice
- 1 3/4 cups water
- 1/2 teaspoon salt

Directions:

1. Combine the rice, water, and 1/2 teaspoon of salt in a medium saucepan. First, bring the water and rice to a boil in a pot. Decrease the heat to low, then cover the pot and let it simmer for 15-20 minutes. The rice is done when it's tender and translucent.

After the rice is cooked, use a fork to gently fluff the grains. This separates them and creates a light and airy texture.

2. To begin, pour coconut oil into a large skillet or Dutch oven. Heat it over medium heat. Add the diced onion and sauté for 5-7 minutes, or until the onion is translucent.

3. Slip the minced garlic and grated ginger into the skillet. Cook them for 1-2 minutes, stirring occasionally, until they release their wonderful aroma.

4. Sprinkle in the garam masala, cumin, coriander, turmeric, and cayenne pepper. Give everything a good stir for about a minute, letting the spices sizzle and release their flavors.

5. Toss the diced tomatoes and vegetable broth into the pan. Let it simmer gently. Once simmering, toss in the rinsed and drained chickpeas, cauliflower florets, and diced sweet potato.

6. Turn down the heat to medium-low and let the curry simmer for 15-20 minutes. Keep an eye on the vegetables and cook until they're tender. For the last few minutes of cooking, toss in the frozen peas and stir it all together.

7. Take the dish off the heat and mix in the chopped cilantro. Taste the curry and adjust seasonings with salt and pepper for perfect flavor.

8. Serve the Vegetable Curry over the cooked basmati rice. Enjoy!

Nutritional breakdown per serving:

Calories: 440 kcal, Protein: 13 grams, Carbohydrates: 67 grams, Fat: 14 grams, Saturated Fat: 8 grams, Cholesterol: 0 milligrams, Sodium: 720 milligrams, Fiber: 11 grams, and Sugar: 8 grams.

ROASTED RED PEPPER AND TOMATO SOUP WITH AVOCADO TOASTS

- Total Time: 45 minutes
- Prep Time: 20 minutes
- Servings: 4

Ingredients:

Soup:

- 3 large red bell peppers, cut in half and with the seeds removed
- 2 tablespoons olive oil
- 1 large onion, diced
- 3 cloves garlic, minced
- 1 (28-ounce) can diced tomatoes
- 2 cups vegetable broth
- 1 teaspoon dried oregano
- 1/2 teaspoon ground cumin
- 1/4 teaspoon red pepper flakes
- Salt and black pepper to taste

Avocado Toasts:

- 4 slices whole-grain bread
- 2 ripe avocados, mashed
- 2 tablespoons fresh lemon juice
- 1/4 teaspoon red pepper flakes
- Salt and black pepper to taste

Directions:

1. To commence with the recipe, start by preheating your oven to 400°F (200°C).
2. Halve and seed them first. Arrange them on a baking sheet, skin facing up. Pop them in your preheated oven for 20-25 minutes, or until the skins get charred and blistered. Once done, take them out and let them cool for 10 minutes.
3. Once the peppers have cooled down sufficiently, peel off and discard the skins. Optionally, roughly chop the roasted pepper flesh.
4. Heat it over medium heat in a large saucepan or Dutch oven. Add the diced onion and sauté for 5-7 minutes, or until the onion is translucent.
5. Let the delicious aroma of the garlic fill the kitchen as you cook it for 1-2 minutes.

6. Stir in the chopped roasted red peppers, canned diced tomatoes, vegetable broth, dried oregano, ground cumin, and red pepper flakes. Bring the mixture to a simmer.
7. Reduce the heat to low and let the soup simmer for 15-20 minutes, stirring occasionally, to allow the flavors to meld.
8. That rewrite is perfect! It conveys the information clearly, avoids plagiarism, and keeps it concise. Be careful when blending hot liquids. Return the blended soup to the saucepan and keep it warm.
9. In a small bowl, mash the avocados with the lemon juice, red pepper flakes, and a pinch of salt and black pepper.
10. Heat the whole-grain bread slices until they reach a golden brown color.
11. To serve, ladle the Roasted Red Pepper and Tomato Soup into bowls. Top each serving with a dollop of the mashed avocado and serve the avocado toasts on the side.

Nutritional breakdown per serving:

Calories: 350 kcal, Protein: 8 grams, Carbohydrates: 42 grams, Fat: 18 grams, Saturated Fat: 2.5 grams, Cholesterol: 0 milligrams, Sodium: 640 milligrams, Fiber: 11 grams, and Sugar: 10 grams.

SEARED AHI TUNA POKE BOWL WITH EDAMAME AND PICKLED GINGER

- Total Time: 30 minutes
- Prep Time: 20 minutes
- Servings: 4

Ingredients:

Poke Bowl:

- 1 lb sushi-grade ahi tuna, cut into 1-inch cubes
- 2 cups cooked brown rice
- 1 cup shelled edamame, steamed
- 1 avocado, diced
- 1 cucumber, diced
- 2 green onions, thinly sliced
- 2 tablespoons toasted sesame seeds

Poke Sauce:

- 3 tablespoons soy sauce
- 2 tablespoons rice vinegar
- 1 tablespoon sesame oil
- 1 tablespoon honey
- 1 teaspoon grated ginger
- 1 teaspoon Sriracha (or to taste)
- 1 teaspoon sesame seeds

Pickled Ginger:

- 1 cup thinly sliced fresh ginger
- 1/2 cup rice vinegar
- 2 tablespoons sugar
- 1/2 teaspoon salt

Directions:

1. Make the pickled ginger: In a small saucepan, combine the sliced ginger, rice vinegar, sugar, and salt. Get the mixture boiling hot, then turn down the heat and simmer for 5 minutes. Remove from heat and let cool completely. Drain the ginger and set aside.

2. In a small bowl, whisk up the soy sauce, rice vinegar, sesame oil, honey, grated ginger, Sriracha, and sesame seeds. This tasty dressing will be waiting on the sidelines for now.

3. Whichever pan you choose, cast-iron or nonstick, preheat it over high heat. Sear the ahi tuna cubes for 1-2 minutes per side, just until the outside is lightly seared but the inside is still rare to medium-rare. Rest easy, the tuna's done! Take it out of the pan and let it sit for a few minutes.

4. Divide the cooked brown rice among 4 serving bowls. Top each bowl with the seared ahi tuna, edamame, diced avocado, diced cucumber, and sliced green onions.

5. Dress your poke bowls with a drizzle of the flavorful poke sauce. Don't forget to sprinkle some toasted sesame seeds on top for an extra crunch!

6. Serve the Seared Ahi Tuna Poke Bowls immediately, garnished with the pickled ginger.

Nutritional breakdown per serving:

Calories: 425 kcal, Protein: 33 grams, Carbohydrates: 42 grams, Fat: 17 grams, Saturated Fat: 3 grams, Cholesterol: 40 milligrams, Sodium: 770 milligrams, Fiber: 7 grams, and Sugar: 8 grams.

LENTIL AND SWEET POTATO SHEPHERD'S PIE

- Total Time: 1 hour 15 minutes
- Prep Time: 30 minutes
- Servings: 6

Ingredients:

Filling:

- 1 cup dried brown lentils, rinsed
- 4 cups vegetable broth
- 1 large sweet potato, peeled and diced
- 1 onion, diced
- 2 carrots, peeled and diced
- 2 celery stalks, diced
- 3 garlic cloves, minced
- 2 tablespoons tomato paste
- 2 teaspoons dried thyme
- 1 teaspoon dried rosemary
- 1/2 teaspoon smoked paprika
- Salt and pepper to taste
- Mashed Sweet Potato Topping:
- 3 large sweet potatoes, chopped into 1-inch pieces
- 2 tablespoons unsalted butter
- 1/4 cup unsweetened almond milk
- 1/2 teaspoon salt

Directions:

1. To commence with the recipe, start by preheating your oven to 375°F (190°C).
2. Toss the lentils and vegetable broth together in a large pot. Bring to a boil first, then reduce heat and simmer 15-20 minutes. Drain any extra liquid and set aside.
3. Heat a little oil in a large skillet or Dutch oven over medium heat. Toss the onion, carrots, and celery in your pan with a bit of oil. Cook over medium heat for 5-7 minutes, stirring now and then, until they're tender. Cook the garlic 1 more minute, giving it a stir every now and then, until it becomes fragrant.
4. Stir in the diced sweet potato, tomato paste, thyme, rosemary, and smoked paprika. Season with salt and pepper to taste. Sauté the sweet potato for 5-7 minutes, stirring every now and then, until it starts to get tender.

5. Toss the cooked lentils in with the veggies and give it a good stir to combine everything. Spread the lentil and vegetable filling into a 9-inch pie dish or baking dish.
6. Simmer the chopped sweet potatoes in a large pot of water until fork-tender, about 15-20 minutes. Drain any excess liquid.
7. Mash sweet potatoes with butter, almond milk, and salt for a creamy and delicious flavor.
8. Spread the mashed sweet potato topping evenly over the lentil and vegetable filling.
9. Bake the Lentil and Sweet Potato Shepherd's Pie in the preheated oven for 30-35 minutes, or until the filling is bubbling and the top is lightly browned.
10. Take the pie out of the oven and let it cool for 10-15 minutes before serving.

Nutritional breakdown per serving:

Calories: 345 kcal, Protein: 12 grams, Carbohydrates: 58 grams, Fat: 7 grams, Saturated Fat: 3 grams, Cholesterol: 10 milligrams, Sodium: 775 milligrams, Fiber: 13 grams, and Sugar: 11 grams.

GRILLED SHRIMP AND ZUCCHINI NOODLE BOWLS WITH PESTO

- Total Time: 35 minutes
- Prep Time: 20 minutes
- Servings: 4

Ingredients:

Pesto:

- 2 cups fresh basil leaves
- 1/4 cup pine nuts
- 2 garlic cloves
- 1/4 cup grated Parmesan cheese
- 1/4 cup olive oil
- 1 tablespoon lemon juice
- 1/4 teaspoon salt

Bowls:

- 1 pound large shrimp, peeled and deveined
- 2 medium zucchini, spiralized or julienned into noodles
- 1 pint cherry tomatoes, halved
- 1/4 cup crumbled feta cheese
- 2 tablespoons toasted pine nuts
- Salt and pepper to taste

Instructions:

1. In your food processor, combine basil leaves, pine nuts, garlic cloves, Parmesan cheese, olive oil, lemon juice, and salt. Blend until completely smooth, achieving a thick sauce-like consistency. Then, set aside.
2. Metal skewers are ready to use. Wooden skewers need a 30-minute soak in water to prevent burning before threading the shrimp. Season the shrimp with salt and pepper.
3. To achieve those beautiful grill marks, preheat your grill or grill pan to medium-high.
4. Grill them for 2-3 minutes per side, until they're completely pink and cooked through. Let them rest briefly off the skewers before serving.
5. Toss together the spiralized zucchini noodles (or julienned zucchini, if preferred) with the grilled shrimp, cherry tomatoes, crumbled feta cheese, and a generous ¼ cup of the prepared pesto.

6. Divide the shrimp and zucchini noodle mixture evenly among 4 serving bowls.
7. Finish each bowl with a sprinkle of toasted pine nuts.
8. Serve immediately, with any remaining pesto on the side for drizzling or dipping.

Nutritional breakdown per serving:

Calories: 365 kcal, Protein: 30 grams, Carbohydrates: 12 grams, Fat: 24 grams, Saturated Fat: 5 grams, Cholesterol: 185 milligrams, Sodium: 630 milligrams, Fiber: 3 grams, and Sugar: 5 grams.

QUINOA AND BLACK BEAN STUFFED BELL PEPPERS

- Total Time: 1 hour
- Prep Time: 20 minutes
- Servings: 6

Ingredients:

- 6 medium bell peppers (any color)
- 1 cup uncooked quinoa, rinsed
- 2 cups vegetable broth
- 1 can black beans, rinsed
- 1 cup frozen corn kernels
- 1 small onion, diced
- 2 cloves garlic, minced
- 1 teaspoon ground cumin
- 1 teaspoon chili powder
- 1/2 teaspoon dried oregano
- 1/4 teaspoon cayenne pepper (optional)
- Salt and black pepper to taste
- 1 cup shredded cheese

Directions:

1. To begin the recipe, initiate by preheating your oven to 375°F (190°C).
2. Hollow out the bell peppers: cut the tops, remove seeds and membranes, then place them in a baking dish.
3. Bring together the quinoa and vegetable broth in a medium saucepan. Increase the heat to bring the mixture to a boil. Once boiling, reduce the heat to low, cover the pot, and simmer for 15-20 minutes. Look for the quinoa to become tender and the liquid to disappear completely. Gently stir the quinoa with a fork to separate the grains. Set aside.
4. Heat a large skillet over medium heat. Add a bit of oil and sauté the diced onion for about 5 minutes, until translucent. After that, mix in the minced garlic and cook for 1 more minute, until aromatic.
5. To the skillet, add the cooked quinoa, black beans, frozen corn, cumin, chili powder, oregano, and cayenne pepper (if using). Customize the flavor with salt and black pepper to your preference, and ensure thorough mixing of the ingredients.
6. Spoon the quinoa and black bean mixture evenly into the hollowed-out bell peppers. Top each stuffed pepper generously with shredded cheese.

7. Bake for 30-35 minutes, or until the peppers have softened and the cheese has melted and begun to bubble. If the dish begins to brown too quickly, you can protect it by covering with aluminum foil.
8. Let the stuffed peppers chill for 5-10 minutes after the oven.

Nutritional breakdown per serving 1 stuffed pepper):

Calories: 310 kcal, Protein: 15 grams, Carbohydrates: 41 grams, Fat: 10 grams, Saturated Fat: 5 grams, Cholesterol: 25 milligrams, Sodium: 540 milligrams, Fiber: 9 grams, and Sugar: 6 grams.

MEDITERRANEAN CHICKEN SALAD WRAPS WITH CUCUMBER AND FETA

- Total Time: 30 minutes
- Prep Time: 20 minutes
- Servings: 4

Ingredients:

Chicken Salad:

- 2 cups cooked, shredded or diced chicken
- 1/2 cup plain Greek yogurt
- 2 tablespoons chopped fresh parsley
- 2 tablespoons chopped fresh basil
- 1 tablespoon lemon juice
- 1 teaspoon Dijon mustard
- 1/4 teaspoon dried oregano
- Salt and pepper to taste

Wraps:

- 4 whole wheat tortillas or wraps
- 1 cup thinly sliced cucumber
- 1/2 cup crumbled feta cheese
- 1/4 cup sliced kalamata olives (optional)

Instructions:

1. In a medium bowl, combine the shredded or diced chicken, Greek yogurt, parsley, basil, lemon juice, Dijon mustard, and dried oregano. Give it a good stir and season with salt and pepper to your liking. Then, set it aside.
2. Lay the tortillas or wraps on a clean surface. Divide the chicken salad evenly among the wraps, spreading it in a line down the center.
3. Top the chicken salad with sliced cucumber, crumbled feta cheese, and sliced kalamata olives (if using).
4. Start by giving the bottom of the wrap a fold over the filling. Tuck in the sides next, and roll the wrap up snugly to keep everything inside.
5. For easy eating, slice each wrap diagonally into halves and serve right away.

Nutritional breakdown per serving:

Calories (1 wrap): 340 kcal, Protein: 26 grams, Carbohydrates: 33 grams, Fat: 13 grams, Saturated Fat: 5 grams, Cholesterol: 65 milligrams, Sodium: 720 milligrams, Fiber: 5 grams, and Sugar: 3 grams.

ROASTED BUTTERNUT SQUASH AND KALE LASAGNA

- Total Time: 1 hour 30 minutes
- Prep Time: 45 minutes
- Servings: 9

Ingredients:

Roasted Butternut Squash:

- 1 medium butternut squash, cubed (about 4 cups)
- 2 tablespoons olive oil
- 1/2 teaspoon salt
- 1/4 teaspoon black pepper

Kale Filling:

- 1 tablespoon olive oil
- 1 small onion, diced
- 3 cloves garlic, minced
- 4 cups chopped kale, stems removed
- 1/4 teaspoon nutmeg
- Salt and pepper to taste

Lasagna:

- 9 lasagna noodles (whole wheat or gluten-free, if desired)
- 1 1/2 cups ricotta cheese
- 1 cup shredded mozzarella cheese
- 1/2 cup grated Parmesan cheese
- 1 egg
- 1/4 teaspoon salt

Instructions:

- To begin the recipe, initiate by preheating your oven to 400°F (200°C). Cover a baking sheet with parchment paper as a preparation step.
- Arrange the cubed butternut squash on the prepared baking sheet. Mix the diced butternut squash with 2 tablespoons of olive oil, 1/2 teaspoon of salt, and 1/4 teaspoon of black pepper in a bowl. Toss to coat everything well. Roast for 25-30

minutes, checking for doneness. You want the squash tender and beautifully browned.

- Get your large skillet hot by heating 1 tablespoon of olive oil over medium heat. Sauté the onions until softened and translucent (about 5 minutes). Sweat the diced onion in the pan, stirring occasionally, until softened. After the onions soften and become translucent (around 5 minutes), toss in the minced garlic. Cook for another minute, letting the delicious aroma waft through the kitchen.

- Toss the chopped kale into the skillet and cook, stirring occasionally, for 3-5 minutes until wilted and tender. Season it with nutmeg, salt, and pepper according to your preferences. Once seasoned, remove the kale mixture from the heat and set it aside.

- Grab a medium bowl and whisk together ricotta cheese, grated Parmesan, a pinch of salt, and an egg until smooth. Gently fold in half the shredded mozzarella until everything is barely combined – a few streaks are okay!

- Spread 1/2 cup of the roasted butternut squash in the bottom of a 9x13-inch baking dish. Start by spreading half of the ricotta cheese mixture on the bottom of your baking dish. Top with 3 lasagna noodles, then evenly distribute half of the kale mixture over the noodles. Repeat this layer one more time.

- Spoon dollops of the remaining ricotta cheese mixture onto the first layer of noodles and kale. Top it with all the roasted butternut squash, followed by the final 3 lasagna noodles.

- Start by tenting the dish with aluminum foil. Bake it for 30 minutes to trap steam and create a moist cooking environment.

- Reveal the lasagna by removing the foil and sprinkle the remaining 1/2 cup of mozzarella cheese on top. Bake for 15 more minutes, or until the cheese is melted and reaches a bubbly golden brown state.

- To ensure perfectly formed slices and a delightful eating experience, allow the lasagna to rest for 10-15 minutes before serving.

Nutritional breakdown per serving:

Calories (1/9 of the lasagna): 330 kcal, Protein: 19 grams, Carbohydrates: 38 grams, Fat: 13 grams, Saturated Fat: 6 grams, Cholesterol: 55 milligrams, Sodium: 520 milligrams, Fiber: 5 grams, and Sugar: 5 grams.

SALMON AND ASPARAGUS FOIL PACKETS WITH DILL SAUCE

- Total Time: 30 minutes
- Prep Time: 15 minutes
- Servings: 4

Ingredients:

Salmon and Asparagus:

- 4 (6-ounce) salmon fillets
- 1 pound asparagus, prepped
- 2 tablespoons olive oil
- 1 teaspoon dried dill
- 1/2 teaspoon garlic powder
- 1/2 teaspoon salt
- 1/4 teaspoon black pepper

Dill Sauce:

- 1/2 cup plain Greek yogurt
- 2 tablespoons chopped fresh dill
- 1 tablespoon lemon juice
- 1 teaspoon Dijon mustard
- 1/4 teaspoon garlic powder
- Salt and pepper to taste

Instructions:

1. The first step is to preheat your oven to the key temperature of 400°F (200°C).
2. Prepare four sheets of heavy-duty aluminum foil, each roughly 12 inches by 18 inches.
3. Place one salmon fillet in the center of each foil sheet. Divide the asparagus pieces evenly among the four packets, placing them next to the salmon.
4. In a small bowl, whisk together the olive oil, dried dill, garlic powder, salt, and black pepper. Drizzle this mixture over the salmon and asparagus in each foil packet, making sure to evenly coat the ingredients.
5. Create a sealed pouch for cooking by folding the foil over the salmon and asparagus, and crimping the edges shut.

6. Nestle the foil packets on a baking sheet and bake for 18-20 minutes for even cooking. The salmon is ready when it has lost its translucency and breaks into flakes when prodded with a fork.
7. Take advantage of the salmon's baking time to prepare the dill sauce. In a small bowl, whisk together a creamy base of Greek yogurt with chopped fresh dill, lemon juice, Dijon mustard, and garlic powder.
8. Once the salmon and asparagus are cooked, carefully open the foil packets (be cautious of the hot steam). Serve the salmon and asparagus immediately, with the dill sauce on the side for dipping or drizzling.

Nutritional breakdown per serving (1 salmon fillet with asparagus and 2 tablespoons of dill sauce):

Calories: 340 kcal, Protein: 39 grams, Carbohydrates: 8 grams, Fat: 16 grams, Saturated Fat: 3 grams, Cholesterol: 90 milligrams, Sodium: 620 milligrams, Fiber: 3 grams, and Sugar: 3 grams.

VEGGIE-PACKED FRIED RICE WITH CASHEWS AND EGGS

- Total Time: 30 minutes
- Prep Time: 15 minutes
- Servings: 4

Ingredients:

- 2 cups cooked brown rice, cooled
- 2 tablespoons sesame oil
- 1 cup diced carrots
- 1 cup diced bell peppers (any color)
- 1 cup diced mushrooms
- 1 cup diced zucchini
- 1/2 cup frozen peas
- 3 cloves garlic, minced
- 1 tablespoon grated fresh ginger
- 2 eggs, lightly beaten
- 1/4 cup unsalted roasted cashews
- 2 tablespoons low-sodium soy sauce
- 1 tablespoon rice vinegar
- 1 teaspoon sesame seeds (optional)
- Salt and black pepper to taste

Instructions:

1. Get your large non-stick skillet or wok nice and hot by heating the sesame oil over **medium**-high heat.
2. Add the diced carrots, bell peppers, mushrooms, and zucchini. Cook the vegetables for 5-7 minutes, stirring them from time to time, until they reach a tender-crisp perfection.
3. Add the frozen peas, minced garlic, and grated ginger. Sauté for an additional 2 minutes, until fragrant.
4. Create a well in the center of the pan by scooping the vegetables towards the edges. Pour the beaten eggs into the well and cook, gently folding them into the vegetables with frequent stirring. Continue until the eggs are no longer runny and appear opaque throughout, about 1-2 minutes.
5. Gently incorporate the cooked brown rice into the pan, using a spatula to loosen and fold everything together. Break up any large clumps of rice as you mix.

6. Stir in the unsalted roasted cashews, soy sauce, and rice vinegar. Finish the dish by adding salt and black pepper to your liking.
7. Enjoy this dish hot, and for an extra touch, sprinkle with sesame seeds.

Nutritional breakdown per serving:

Calories (1/4 of the recipe): 330 kcal, Protein: 12 grams, Carbohydrates: 42 grams, Fat: 14 grams, Saturated Fat: 2 grams, Cholesterol: 93 milligrams, Sodium: 420 milligrams, Fiber: 5 grams, and Sugar: 4 grams.

CHICKPEA AND AVOCADO LETTUCE WRAPS WITH TAHINI DRESSING

- Total Time: 25 minutes
- Prep Time: 15 minutes
- Servings: 4

Ingredients:

Chickpea and Avocado Filling:

- 1 (15-ounce) can chickpeas, drained and rinsed
- 1 avocado, diced
- 1/2 cup diced cucumber
- 1/4 cup diced red onion
- 2 tablespoons chopped fresh parsley
- 1 tablespoon lemon juice
- 1 teaspoon ground cumin
- 1/4 teaspoon salt
- 1/8 teaspoon black pepper

Tahini Dressing:

- 1/4 cup tahini
- 2 tablespoons warm water
- 1 tablespoon lemon juice
- 1 tablespoon honey
- 1 garlic clove, minced
- 1/4 teaspoon salt

Lettuce Wraps:

- 12 large romaine lettuce leaves, freshly rinsed and dried

Instructions:

1. In a medium bowl, toss together all the chickpea and avocado filling ingredients until well combined.
2. In a small bowl, whisk together all the tahini dressing ingredients until smooth and creamy.
3. Place a few tablespoons of the chickpea and avocado filling in the center of each romaine lettuce leaf.
4. Drizzle the tahini dressing over the filling, dividing it evenly among the lettuce wraps.

5. Fill each lettuce leaf with the chickpea and avocado mixture, then fold or wrap them to create delicious handheld treats. Serve immediately.

Nutritional breakdown per serving (3 lettuce wraps):

Calories: 290 kcal, Protein: 10 grams, Carbohydrates: 32 grams, Fat: 15 grams, Saturated Fat: 2 grams, Cholesterol: 0 milligrams, Sodium: 390 milligrams, Fiber: 9 grams, and Sugar: 10 grams.

TURKEY AND SWEET POTATO STUFFED PORTOBELLO MUSHROOMS

- Total Time: 45 minutes
- Prep Time: 20 minutes
- Servings: 4 (2 mushroom caps per serving)

Ingredients:

- 8 large portobello mushrooms, prepped (stems removed and chopped)
- 1 tablespoon olive oil
- 1 pound ground turkey
- 1 cup diced sweet potato
- 1/2 cup diced onion
- 2 garlic cloves, minced
- 1 teaspoon dried thyme
- 1/2 teaspoon ground cumin
- 1/4 teaspoon cayenne pepper
- 1/4 teaspoon salt
- 1/8 teaspoon black pepper
- 1/2 cup shredded mozzarella cheese
- 2 tablespoons chopped fresh parsley (for garnish)

Instructions:

1. Preheat your oven to the key temperature of 400°F (200°C) to begin.
2. Gently clean the portobello mushroom caps with a damp paper towel, and remove the stems. Chop the stems and set them aside.
3. In a large skillet, heat the olive oil over medium-high heat. Add the chopped mushroom stems, ground turkey, diced sweet potato, onion, and garlic. Sauté the mixture, breaking up the turkey with a spatula, until the turkey is nicely browned and the sweet potatoes are tender throughout, about 8-10 minutes.
4. Stir in the dried thyme, cumin, cayenne pepper, salt, and black pepper. Taste and adjust the seasoning as needed.
5. Arrange the portobello mushroom caps, gill-side up, on a baking sheet lined with parchment paper.
6. Scoop the turkey and sweet potato mixture evenly into the mushroom caps, pressing it down gently to create a flat, even surface.
7. Generously coat the stuffed mushrooms with shredded mozzarella cheese, creating a visually appealing blanket that will melt to gooey perfection.

8. Bake uncovered for 20-25 minutes, letting the cheese bubble and the mushrooms soften to perfection.
9. Carefully take the stuffed mushrooms out of the oven and add a finishing touch with a sprinkle of chopped fresh parsley.

Nutritional breakdown per serving (2 mushroom caps):

Calories: 280 kcal, Protein: 25 grams, Carbohydrates: 17 grams, Fat: 13 grams, Saturated Fat: 4 grams, Cholesterol: 75 milligrams, Sodium: 330 milligrams, Fiber: 3 grams, and Sugar: 4 grams.

GRILLED CHICKEN AND MANGO SALAD WITH HONEY-LIME VINAIGRETTE

- Total Time: 30 minutes
- Prep Time: 20 minutes
- Servings: 4

Ingredients:

Salad:

- 4 boneless, skinless chicken breasts
- 1 teaspoon olive oil
- 1/4 teaspoon salt
- 1/8 teaspoon black pepper
- 8 cups mixed greens (such as spinach, arugula, and romaine)
- 1 ripe mango, peeled and diced
- 1/2 cup diced red bell pepper
- 1/4 cup thinly sliced red onion

Honey-Lime Vinaigrette:

- 2 tablespoons olive oil
- 2 tablespoons fresh lime juice
- 1 tablespoon honey
- 1 teaspoon Dijon mustard
- 1/4 teaspoon salt
- 1/8 teaspoon black pepper

Instructions:

1. For a restaurant-quality sear, preheat your grill or grill pan to scorching hot over medium-high heat.
2. Brush chicken with 1 tsp olive oil, season generously with fresh black pepper and salt (to taste).
3. Grill them for 5-7 minutes a side, flipping once, until they hit 165°F (74°C) internally for food safety. This will lock in the juices for a more flavorful and tender result. Let chicken rest 5 minutes on cutting board (redistributes juices).
4. Combine the honey-lime vinaigrette ingredients in a small bowl: olive oil, fresh lime juice, a touch of honey, Dijon mustard for a tangy kick, and a pinch of salt and black pepper.

81

5. Create a colorful salad by tossing together mixed greens, diced mango for a burst of sunshine, vibrant red bell pepper squares, and thinly sliced red onion in a large bowl.
6. Thinly slice the grilled chicken breasts and arrange them artfully over the salad in the bowl.
7. Drizzle the honey-lime vinaigrette over the salad and gently toss to coat the ingredients evenly.
8. Serve the Grilled Chicken and Mango Salad immediately, with any additional vinaigrette on the side.

Nutritional breakdown per serving:

Calories: 360 kcal, Protein: 36 grams, Carbohydrates: 25 grams, Fat: 14 grams, Saturated Fat: 2 grams, Cholesterol: 95 milligrams, Sodium: 420 milligrams, Fiber: 5 grams, and Sugar: 18 grams.

SPICY LENTIL AND VEGETABLE SOUP WITH WHOLE GRAIN CRACKERS

- Total Time: 60 minutes
- Prep Time: 20 minutes
- Servings: 6

Ingredients:

Soup:

- 1 tablespoon olive oil
- 1 yellow onion, diced
- 3 garlic cloves, minced
- 1 tablespoon grated fresh ginger
- 1 teaspoon ground cumin
- 1 teaspoon paprika
- 1/2 teaspoon red pepper flakes
- 1 cup dried brown lentils, rinsed
- 4 cups low-sodium vegetable broth
- 1 (14.5 oz) can diced tomatoes
- 2 cups diced carrots
- 1 cup diced celery
- 1 cup diced zucchini
- 1 teaspoon salt
- 1/4 teaspoon black pepper

Whole Grain Crackers:

- 1 cup whole wheat flour
- 1/2 cup rolled oats
- 1/2 teaspoon baking powder
- 1/4 teaspoon salt
- 3 tablespoons cold unsalted butter, cubed
- 3-4 tablespoons cold water

Instructions:

1. For this recipe, grab a large pot or Dutch oven. Heat olive oil over medium heat to get started. Once hot, add the diced onion and sauté for 5-7 minutes, until it becomes translucent.

2. Add the minced garlic, grated ginger, cumin, paprika, and red pepper flakes. Sauté the spices for 1 minute, stirring constantly, to release their fragrant oils and awaken their flavor.
3. Stir in the rinsed lentils, vegetable broth, diced tomatoes, carrots, celery, and zucchini. Season with salt and black pepper.
4. Bring soup to a boil, then simmer 30-35 minutes until lentils and vegetables are tender.
5. Sample the soup and adjust seasonings (salt & pepper) for a perfectly balanced flavor.
6. The first thing you should do is preheat your oven to 375°F (190°C). Cover a baking sheet with parchment paper as a preparation step.
7. Whisk whole wheat flour, rolled oats, baking powder, and salt together in a medium bowl.
8. Using fingers or pastry cutter, break cold butter into dry ingredients until crumbly. This creates air pockets for a light and flaky final product.
9. Add the cold water, 1 tablespoon at a time, and mix until a dough forms.
10. For even baking, use a rolling pin to roll out the dough on a lightly floured surface until it reaches a consistent thickness of ⅛ inch. Unleash your creativity and cut out your desired cracker shapes using cookie cutters or a sharp knife.
11. Place crackers on the baking sheet, leaving 1 inch between each.
12. Bake the crackers for 12-15 minutes, or until they turn a beautiful golden brown and are crisp throughout. Keep an eye on them to ensure they don't burn. Allow them to cool completely before serving.

Nutritional breakdown per serving:

Calories (1 cup of soup and 4 crackers): 290 kcal, Protein: 14 grams, Carbohydrates: 46 grams, Fat: 7 grams, Saturated Fat: 2 grams, Cholesterol: 5 milligrams, Sodium: 590 milligrams, Fiber: 13 grams, and Sugar: 6 grams.

ROASTED CAULIFLOWER AND QUINOA BOWL WITH TAHINI DRESSING

- Total Time: 45 minutes
- Prep Time: 15 minutes
- Servings: 4

Ingredients:

Roasted Cauliflower:

- 4 cups cauliflower florets
- 2 tablespoons olive oil
- 1/2 teaspoon garlic powder
- 1/2 teaspoon paprika
- 1/4 teaspoon salt
- 1/8 teaspoon black pepper

Quinoa:

- 1 cup uncooked quinoa, rinsed
- 2 cups low-sodium vegetable broth

Tahini Dressing:

- 1/4 cup tahini
- 2 tablespoons freshly squeezed lemon juice
- 1 garlic clove, minced
- 2 tablespoons water
- 1 tablespoon honey
- 1/4 teaspoon salt
- 1/8 teaspoon black pepper

Bowl Components:

- 1 cup baby spinach
- 1 avocado, diced
- 2 tablespoons toasted sesame seeds
- 2 tablespoons chopped fresh parsley

Instructions:

1. Adjust your oven's thermostat to 400°F (200°C) in preparation for preheating. Line a baking sheet with parchment paper.
2. For even seasoning, toss the cauliflower florets in a large bowl with olive oil, garlic powder, paprika, salt, and black pepper. Use your hands or a large spoon to ensure each floret is coated in the flavorful mixture.
3. Scatter the seasoned cauliflower florets on a baking sheet, forming a single layer. This ensures even heating and browning on all sides.
4. Roast the cauliflower florets for 20-25 minutes, or until they become fork-tender for a melt-in-your-mouth experience. Don't forget to flip them halfway through for even browning.
5. To begin, combine the rinsed quinoa and vegetable broth in a medium saucepan.
6. Bring the mixture to a boil, then reduce the heat to low, cover, and simmer for 15-18 minutes, or until the quinoa is tender and the liquid is absorbed.
7. Fluff the cooked quinoa with a fork.
8. To make the tahini sauce, whisk together tahini, lemon juice, minced garlic, water (for desired consistency), honey (for a touch of sweetness), salt, and black pepper in a small bowl until smooth and creamy.
9. Divide the cooked quinoa evenly among 4 serving bowls.
10. Top each bowl with roasted cauliflower florets, baby spinach, diced avocado, toasted sesame seeds, and chopped fresh parsley.
11. Drizzle the tahini dressing over the bowls and serve immediately.

Nutritional breakdown per serving:

Calories: 425 kcal, Protein: 13 grams, Carbohydrates: 46 grams, Fat: 23 grams, Saturated Fat: 3 grams, Cholesterol: 0 milligrams, Sodium: 480 milligrams, Fiber: 12 grams, and Sugar: 8 grams.

BAKED COD WITH MANGO SALSA AND ROASTED BROCCOLI

- Total Time: 45 minutes
- Prep Time: 20 minutes
- Servings: 4

Ingredients:

Mango Salsa:

- 1 ripe mango, diced (about 1 cup)
- 1/4 cup finely chopped red onion
- 1 jalapeño, seeded and finely chopped (about 1 tablespoon)
- 2 tablespoons freshly squeezed lime juice
- 2 tablespoons chopped fresh cilantro
- 1/4 teaspoon salt

Baked Cod:

- 4 (6-ounce) cod fillets
- 2 tablespoons olive oil
- 1 teaspoon garlic powder
- 1 teaspoon paprika
- 1/2 teaspoon salt
- 1/4 teaspoon black pepper

Roasted Broccoli:

- 4 cups broccoli florets
- 2 tablespoons olive oil
- 1/2 teaspoon garlic powder
- 1/4 teaspoon salt
- 1/8 teaspoon black pepper

Instructions:

1. In a medium bowl, combine the diced mango, red onion, jalapeño, lime juice, cilantro, and salt. Stir well to combine. Cover and refrigerate until ready to serve.
2. Initiate by setting your oven to preheat at 400°F (200°C) as the first step. Cover a baking sheet with parchment paper as a preparation step.
3. Space cod fillets on the baking sheet for even cooking. Lightly coat the cod fillets with olive oil for moisture. Then, sprinkle them generously with garlic powder, paprika,

salt, and black pepper, gently rubbing the seasoning mixture into the fish for maximum flavor.

4. Bake for 12-15 minutes, or until the cod is opaque and flakes easily with a fork.
5. Toss the broccoli florets in a large bowl with olive oil, garlic powder, a sprinkle of salt, and a pinch of red pepper flakes for a touch of heat.
6. To promote even roasting and browning, spread the seasoned broccoli florets out in a single layer on a separate baking sheet.
7. Roast for 15-18 minutes, or until the broccoli is tender and lightly charred, flipping halfway through.
8. Divide the roasted broccoli evenly among 4 plates.
9. Place a baked cod fillet on top of the broccoli on each plate.
10. Top the cod with a generous portion of the mango salsa.
11. Serve immediately.

Nutritional breakdown per serving:

Calories: 350 kcal, Protein: 36 grams, Carbohydrates: 22 grams, Fat: 14 grams, Saturated Fat: 2 grams, Cholesterol: 70 milligrams, Sodium: 650 milligrams, Fiber: 5 grams, and Sugar: 9 grams.

ZUCCHINI NOODLE PAD THAI WITH SHRIMP

- Total Time: 35 minutes
- Prep Time: 20 minutes
- Servings: 4

Ingredients:

Zucchini Noodles:

- 3 medium zucchinis, spiralized or julienned (about 4 cups)
- Pad Thai Sauce:
- 3 tablespoons fish sauce
- 2 tablespoons lime juice
- 2 tablespoons brown sugar
- 1 tablespoon low-sodium soy sauce
- 1 teaspoon chili garlic sauce
- 1 teaspoon sesame oil

Stir-Fry:

- 1 tablespoon coconut oil
- 1 pound large shrimp, peeled and deveined
- 2 cloves garlic, minced
- 2 eggs, lightly beaten
- 2 cups mung bean sprouts
- 2 green onions, sliced
- 2 tablespoons chopped roasted peanuts
- 2 tablespoons chopped fresh cilantro

Instructions:

1. Spiralize or julienne zucchini into thin noodles (set aside).
2. Mix fish sauce, lime juice, brown sugar, soy sauce, chili garlic sauce, and sesame oil (dressing, set aside).
3. In a large skillet or wok, heat the coconut oil over medium-high heat.
4. Sauté the shrimp and garlic together for 2-3 minutes, or until the shrimp turn opaque and slightly curl, indicating they're cooked through.
5. Push the shrimp to the side of the pan, and pour in the beaten eggs. Scramble the eggs for 1-2 minutes, then mix them with the shrimp.

6. Add the zucchini noodles and Pad Thai sauce to the pan. Toss everything together and cook for 2-3 minutes, or until the noodles are slightly softened and the sauce has thickened.
7. Remove from heat and stir in the mung bean sprouts, green onions, peanuts, and cilantro.
8. Serve immediately.

Nutritional breakdown per serving:

Calories: 265 kcal, Protein: 22 grams, Carbohydrates: 22 grams, Fat: 10 grams, Saturated Fat: 4 grams, Cholesterol: 170 milligrams, Sodium: 860 milligrams, Fiber: 4 grams, and Sugar: 8 grams.

CHICKEN AND VEGETABLE STIR-FRY WITH BROWN RICE

- Total Time: 45 minutes
- Prep Time: 25 minutes
- Servings: 4

Ingredients:

Stir-Fry:

- 1-inch cubed boneless, skinless chicken breasts (1 lb)
- 2 tablespoons sesame oil
- 3 cloves garlic, minced
- 1 tablespoon grated fresh ginger
- 1 red bell pepper, sliced
- 1 cup broccoli florets
- 1 cup snow peas, trimmed
- 1 cup sliced mushrooms
- 1 cup shredded carrots
- 2 green onions, sliced (including green parts)

Sauce:

- 3 tablespoons low-sodium soy sauce
- 2 tablespoons rice vinegar
- 1 tablespoon honey
- 1 teaspoon cornstarch
- Brown Rice:
- 1 cup uncooked brown rice
- 2 cups low-sodium chicken broth

Instructions:

1. Start by adding the brown rice and chicken broth to a medium saucepan. Bring the mixture to a boil, then reduce heat to low, cover the pot, and simmer for 25-30 minutes. This allows the rice to cook gently, absorbing the flavorful liquid and reaching a fluffy, tender texture. Fluff with a fork and set aside.
2. For a sweet and savory sauce, whisk together soy sauce, rice vinegar, a touch of honey, and cornstarch in a small bowl. Set aside until ready to use.
3. Heat sesame oil (high heat) in a large skillet/wok until shimmering.

4. Add the chicken to the hot sesame oil and cook, stirring occasionally, for 3-4 minutes. You're aiming for a nice golden brown sear on all sides.
5. Sauté the garlic and ginger for 1 minute, giving them a good stir to avoid burning.
6. Add the bell pepper, broccoli, snow peas, mushrooms, and carrots. Stir-fry for 5-7 minutes, or until the vegetables are tender-crisp.
7. Add sauce to pan, stir to coat chicken/veggies. Bring to a simmer and cook for 2-3 minutes, or until the sauce thickens to your desired consistency (slightly thickened or nappe-like).
8. Take the pan off the heat and stir in the green onions for a pop of fresh color and a delightful oniony bite.
9. Divide the cooked brown rice evenly among 4 plates.
10. Top the rice with the chicken and vegetable stir-fry.

Nutritional breakdown per serving:

Calories: 425 kcal, Protein: 34 grams, Carbohydrates: 51 grams, Fat: 11 grams, Saturated Fat: 2 grams, Cholesterol: 75 milligrams, Sodium: 560 milligrams, Fiber: 6 grams, and Sugar: 8 grams.

TUSCAN WHITE BEAN AND KALE SOUP

- Total Time: 60 minutes
- Prep Time: 20 minutes
- Servings: 6

Ingredients:

- 2 tablespoons olive oil
- 1 medium yellow onion, diced
- 3 cloves garlic, minced
- 2 carrots, peeled and diced
- 2 celery stalks, diced
- 1 teaspoon dried oregano
- 1 teaspoon dried thyme
- 1/4 teaspoon crushed red pepper flakes
- 4 cups low-sodium chicken or vegetable broth
- 2 cans (15 oz) rinsed & drained cannellini beans
- 1 (14.5-ounce) can diced tomatoes
- 4 cups chopped kale, stems removed
- 1/4 cup grated Parmesan (more for serving)
- Salt & pepper to taste
- Crusty bread, for serving (optional)

Instructions:

1. Heat 1 tbsp olive oil (medium) in a large pot. Sauté onion 5 minutes (softened & translucent). This step helps to build the base flavor for your dish.
2. Toss in the garlic, carrots, and celery with the softened onion. This will add another layer of savory goodness to your dish. Sauté for 5 more minutes, stirring frequently, until the vegetables become tender and fragrant.
3. Stir in the oregano, thyme, and crushed red pepper flakes (if using). Cook for 1 minute, or until fragrant.
4. Pour in the broth, cannellini beans, and diced tomatoes. Bring the mixture to a boil. Simmer 20 minutes (low heat) until veggies soften and liquid reduces.
5. Add the chopped kale to the pot and continue to simmer for 10-15 minutes, or until the kale is tender.
6. Take the pot off the heat and stir in the grated Parmesan cheese until it's fully incorporated and melted throughout the simmered vegetables.
7. Serve the soup hot, with additional Parmesan cheese and crusty bread, if desired.

Nutritional breakdown per serving:

Calories: 279 kcal, Protein: 14 grams, Carbohydrates: 40 grams, Fat: 7 grams, Saturated Fat: 2 grams, Cholesterol: 5 milligrams, Sodium: 641 milligrams, Fiber: 10 grams, and Sugar: 6 grams.

GRILLED SALMON AND ASPARAGUS NIÇOISE SALAD

- Total Time: 40 minutes
- Prep Time: 20 minutes
- Servings: 4

Ingredients:

Salad:

- 1 pound asparagus, trimmed and cut into 1-inch pieces
- 1 pound salmon fillets, skin removed
- 1 tablespoon olive oil
- Salt and freshly ground black pepper
- 4 cups salad greens
- 1 cup halved cherry tomatoes
- 1/2 cup pitted Kalamata olives, halved
- 2 hard-boiled eggs, peeled and quartered

Dressing:

- 1/4 cup red wine vinegar
- 2 tablespoons Dijon mustard
- 1 tablespoon honey
- 1/4 cup olive oil
- Season with salt and pepper

Instructions:

1. Heat up your grill or grill pan. Crank it to medium-high for a good sear!
2. Toss the asparagus in a large bowl with 1 tablespoon of olive oil. Give them a good sprinkle of salt and pepper for extra flavor.
3. Throw the asparagus on the grill and cook for 5-7 minutes, turning them every now and then. Transfer the grilled asparagus to a plate and set aside.
4. Prep the salmon by seasoning it with salt and pepper.
5. In a small bowl, whip up a tangy vinaigrette. Whisk together red wine vinegar, Dijon mustard, a touch of honey, and some olive oil (¼ cup to be exact). Season with salt and pepper. Taste and adjust as needed!
6. Combine red wine vinegar, Dijon mustard, honey, and ¼ cup olive oil in a small bowl. Whisk well to emulsify, then season with salt and pepper to taste.

7. Start with the mixed greens, then add cherry tomatoes, Kalamata olives, hard-boiled egg quarters, and top it all off with the grilled asparagus.
8. Flake the grilled salmon into large chunks and add it to the salad bowl.
9. Give the salad a nice drizzle of the dressing and toss gently to make sure everything gets a flavorful coat!
10. Serve the Grilled Salmon and Asparagus Niçoise Salad immediately.

Nutritional breakdown per serving:

Calories: 418 kcal, Protein: 37 grams, Carbohydrates: 15 grams, Fat: 25 grams, Saturated Fat: 4 grams, Cholesterol: 160 milligrams, Sodium: 581 milligrams, Fiber: 5 grams, and Sugar: 8 grams.

BUTTERNUT SQUASH AND SPINACH LASAGNA ROLLS

- Total Time: 1 hour 30 minutes
- Prep Time: 45 minutes
- Servings: 8

Ingredients:

Filling:

- 2 cups butternut squash, chopped
- 1 tablespoon olive oil
- 1/2 teaspoon salt
- 1/4 teaspoon black pepper
- 10 oz thawed, drained frozen chopped spinach
- 1 cup ricotta cheese
- 1/2 cup grated Parmesan cheese
- 1 egg
- 1 clove garlic, minced
- 1/4 teaspoon ground nutmeg

Lasagna Rolls:

- 8 cooked lasagna noodles
- 2 cups marinara sauce
- 1 cup shredded mozzarella cheese

Instructions:

1. Initiate by setting your oven to preheat at 400°F (200°C) as the first step.
2. Toss the cubed butternut squash with olive oil, a pinch of salt, and some black pepper in a baking dish. Get it ready to go into your preheated oven for some delicious roasting. Roast 20-25 minutes (tender & caramelized). Set aside to cool.
3. In a food processor, blend the roasted butternut squash until smooth.
4. Gather your ingredients in a medium bowl: butternut squash puree, thawed and squeezed spinach, ricotta cheese, Parmesan cheese, an egg, garlic, and nutmeg. Mix everything thoroughly, then set it aside.
5. Reduce the oven temperature to 375°F.
6. Spread about 1/4 cup of the butternut squash and spinach filling onto each cooked lasagna noodle. Carefully roll up the noodle and place it seam-side down in a 9x13-inch baking dish.

7. Coat the lasagna rolls in marinara sauce and then generously sprinkle mozzarella cheese over them.
8. Bake for 30-35 minutes, or until the cheese is golden brown and gooey.
9. Let the lasagna rolls rest for 5-10 minutes out of the oven before serving.

Nutritional breakdown per serving:

Calories: 297 kcal, Protein: 16 grams, Carbohydrates: 31 grams, Fat: 12 grams, Saturated Fat: 5 grams, Cholesterol: 50 milligrams, Sodium: 643 milligrams, Fiber: 5 grams, and Sugar: 6 grams.

THAI COCONUT CURRY WITH SHRIMP AND CAULIFLOWER RICE

- Total Time: 40 minutes
- Prep Time: 20 minutes
- Servings: 4

Ingredients:

Curry:

- 1 tablespoon coconut oil
- 1 small onion, diced
- 3 cloves garlic, minced
- 1 tablespoon grated fresh ginger
- 1 tablespoon red curry paste
- 1 cup coconut milk
- 1 cup low-sodium chicken or vegetable broth
- 1 pound peeled and deveined shrimp
- 1 red bell pepper, sliced
- 2 cups chopped cauliflower florets
- 1 tablespoon fish sauce
- 1 tablespoon lime juice
- 1/4 cup chopped fresh cilantro
- Salt & freshly ground pepper to taste

Cauliflower Rice:

- 4 cups riced cauliflower (about 1 medium head of cauliflower)
- 1 tablespoon coconut oil
- Salt & pepper to taste

Instructions:

1. Warm up 1 tablespoon coconut oil in your large skillet or wok.
2. Add the diced onion and sauté for 2-3 minutes, until translucent.
3. Sauté the garlic and ginger for 1 minute, stirring occasionally. You'll know they're ready when they become fragrant.
4. Introduce the red curry paste to the pan. Cook for 1 minute, stirring occasionally, to release the aromatics.
5. Next, create the base by simmering your preferred broth, chicken or vegetable, with the coconut milk for 5 minutes.

6. Next, add the succulent shrimp, vibrant red bell pepper slices, and chopped cauliflower florets to the pot. Simmer for 5-7 minutes, or until the shrimp is cooked through and the vegetables are tender.
7. For a touch of umami and brightness, stir in the fish sauce and lime juice. Adjust the salt and pepper to create the perfect flavor for you.
8. For a final touch of freshness, swirl in the chopped fresh cilantro after removing the curry from the heat.
9. Break down the cauliflower florets in the food processor with short bursts until they reach a rice-like texture.
10. Prepare a separate pan by heating 1 tablespoon of coconut oil over medium heat.
11. Sauté the riced cauliflower in the pan for 5-7 minutes, stirring occasionally, until it reaches a tender texture.
12. Season the cauliflower rice with salt and black pepper to taste.
13. Divide the cauliflower rice among four bowls.
14. Top each portion of cauliflower rice with the Thai coconut curry with shrimp.
15. Garnish with additional chopped cilantro, if desired.

Nutritional breakdown per serving:

Calories: 359 kcal, Protein: 28 grams, Carbohydrates: 18 grams, Fat: 18 grams, Saturated Fat: 12 grams, Cholesterol: 179 milligrams, Sodium: 682 milligrams, Fiber: 5 grams, and Sugar: 6 grams.

ROASTED VEGETABLE AND HUMMUS FLATBREAD

- Total Time: 40 minutes
- Prep Time: 20 minutes
- Servings: 4

Ingredients:

Roasted Vegetables:

- 1 zucchini, 1/2-inch rounds
- 1 red bell pepper, sliced 1-inch
- 1 cup mushrooms, sliced
- 1 tablespoon olive oil
- 1/2 teaspoon salt
- 1/4 teaspoon black pepper

Flatbread:

- 4 whole-wheat flatbreads or naan
- 1 cup prepared hummus
- 1/4 cup crumbled feta cheese
- 2 tablespoons chopped fresh parsley

Instructions:

1. Initiate by setting your oven to preheat at 400°F (200°C) as the first step.
2. Toss zucchini, peppers, mushrooms with olive oil, salt, pepper on a large sheet pan.
3. Roast veggies 18-20 minutes, stirring halfway, until tender-crisp.
4. Take the roasted vegetables out of the oven. Let them cool on a plate.
5. Place the whole-wheat flatbreads or naan on a clean work surface.
6. Generously spread a 1/4 cup of hummus on each flatbread, leaving a thin rim around the outside.
7. Divide the roasted vegetables evenly among the flatbreads, arranging them in an even layer over the hummus.
8. Crumble feta cheese and scatter it over the roasted vegetables.
9. Place the flatbreads with the toppings on a baking sheet.
10. Bake for 8-10 minutes, watching for melted cheese and a golden brown crust.
11. Let the flatbreads cool slightly for 2-3 minutes before serving.
12. Garnish the flatbreads with a sprinkle of chopped fresh parsley.
13. Cut each flatbread into 4 equal slices and serve.

Nutritional breakdown per serving:

Calories (1 flatbread slice): 226 kcal, Protein: 8 grams, Carbohydrates: 27 grams, Fat: 10 grams, Saturated Fat: 2 grams, Cholesterol: 9 milligrams, Sodium: 508 milligrams, Fiber: 5 grams, and Sugar: 3 grams.

CHICKEN AND AVOCADO SALAD WITH CITRUS VINAIGRETTE

- Total Time: 30 minutes
- Prep Time: 20 minutes
- Servings: 4

Ingredients:

Salad:

- 4 cups mixed greens (baby spinach, arugula, kale)
- 2 cups shredded cooked chicken breast
- 1 avocado, diced
- 1 cup cherry tomatoes, halved
- 1/2 cup thinly sliced cucumber
- 1/4 cup thinly sliced red onion

Citrus Vinaigrette:

- 2 tablespoons fresh orange juice
- 1 tablespoon fresh lemon juice
- 1 tablespoon olive oil
- 1 teaspoon Dijon mustard
- 1 teaspoon honey
- 1/4 teaspoon salt
- 1/8 teaspoon black pepper

Instructions:

1. In a big bowl, assemble the salad with your mixed greens, shredded chicken, diced avocado, cherry tomatoes, cucumber ribbons, and a touch of red onion. Let it wait until you're ready.
2. In a small bowl, whisk together the orange juice, lemon juice, olive oil, Dijon mustard, honey, salt, and black pepper to make the citrus vinaigrette.
3. To finish the salad, give it a light toss with the citrus vinaigrette just before serving. This ensures everything gets evenly coated.
4. Serve the Chicken and Avocado Salad immediately.

Nutritional breakdown per serving:

Calories: 321 kcal, Protein: 26 grams, Carbohydrates: 14 grams, Fat: 18 grams, Saturated Fat: 3 grams, Cholesterol: 63 milligrams, Sodium: 366 milligrams, Fiber: 6 grams, and Sugar: 6 grams.

BAKED FALAFEL WITH CUCUMBER-TOMATO SALAD AND TAHINI

- Total Time: 45 minutes
- Prep Time: 20 minutes
- Servings: 4

Ingredients:

<u>Baked Falafel:</u>

- 15 oz chickpeas, drained and rinsed
- 1/2 cup fresh parsley, chopped
- 1/4 cup fresh cilantro, chopped
- 2 cloves garlic, minced
- 1 teaspoon ground cumin
- 1/2 teaspoon ground coriander
- 1/4 teaspoon baking soda
- 1/4 teaspoon salt
- 1/8 teaspoon black pepper
- 1 tablespoon olive oil

<u>Cucumber-Tomato Salad:</u>

- 1 cup diced cucumber
- 1 cup cherry tomatoes, halved
- 1/4 cup diced red onion
- 2 tablespoons chopped fresh parsley
- 1 tablespoon olive oil
- 1 tablespoon lemon juice
- 1/4 teaspoon salt
- 1/8 teaspoon black pepper

<u>Tahini Sauce:</u>

- 1/4 cup tahini
- 2 tablespoons water
- 1 tablespoon lemon juice
- 1 garlic clove, minced
- 1/4 teaspoon salt

Instructions:

1. Initiate by setting your oven to preheat at 400°F (200°C) as the first step. Cover a baking sheet with parchment paper as a preparation step.
2. Process the chickpeas, parsley, cilantro, garlic, cumin, coriander, baking soda, salt, and black pepper in a food processor until it reaches a coarse texture.
3. Mix in the olive oil with the falafel mixture in a bowl until well incorporated.
4. Scoop the falafel mixture by the tablespoonful and shape into small patties, about 1-inch thick.
5. Arrange the falafel patties on the prepared baking sheet.
6. Bake for 18-20 minutes, flipping halfway, until golden brown and crispy.
7. Cucumber-Tomato Salad:
8. Toss together the diced cucumber, cherry tomatoes, red onion, and chopped parsley in a medium bowl.
9. Lightly toss the salad with olive oil, lemon juice, salt, and pepper to distribute the flavors evenly.
10. In a small bowl, whisk together tahini, water, lemon juice, garlic, and salt until a smooth and creamy sauce forms.
11. Arrange the baked falafel patties on a serving plate.
12. Top with the cucumber-tomato salad.
13. Finish the dish by drizzling the tahini sauce over the falafel and salad.
14. Serve immediately.

Nutritional breakdown per serving:

Calories: 351 kcal, Protein: 12 grams, Carbohydrates: 36 grams, Fat: 20 grams, Saturated Fat: 3 grams, Cholesterol: 0 milligrams, Sodium: 593 milligrams, Fiber: 10 grams, and Sugar: 5 grams.

GRILLED CHICKEN AND STRAWBERRY SALAD WITH BALSAMIC GLAZE

- Total Time: 40 minutes
- Prep Time: 20 minutes
- Servings: 4

Ingredients:

Salad:

- 8 cups mixed greens (e.g., spinach, arugula, and spring mix)
- 1 lb boneless, skinless chicken breasts
- 1 pint fresh strawberries, hulled and halved
- 1/2 cup crumbled feta cheese
- 1/4 cup toasted sliced almonds
- Balsamic Glaze:
- 1/2 cup balsamic vinegar
- 2 tablespoons honey
- 1/4 teaspoon salt

Instructions:

1. Heat balsamic vinegar, honey, and salt in a small saucepan.
2. Simmer the balsamic vinegar, honey, and salt over medium heat, stirring now and then. Reduce the mixture by half until it thickens to a syrupy glaze, about 10-12 minutes. Let it cool before using.
3. Get your grill or grill pan sizzling hot by preheating it to medium-high.
4. Give the chicken breasts a generous seasoning of salt and pepper.
5. Grill the chicken for 5-7 minutes per side, turning once, until cooked through. Let the chicken rest for 5 minutes to lock in the juices. Then, slice or chop it as you prefer.
6. Build your salad in a large bowl with mixed greens, grilled chicken slices, halved strawberries, crumbled feta cheese, and toasted almonds.
7. Finish the salad by drizzling the balsamic glaze on top and gently tossing to coat everything evenly.
8. Serve the Grilled Chicken and Strawberry Salad immediately.

Nutritional breakdown per serving:

Calories: 341 kcal, Protein: 34 grams, Carbohydrates: 21 grams, Fat: 15 grams, Saturated Fat: 5 grams, Cholesterol: 81 milligrams, Sodium: 502 milligrams, Fiber: 4 grams, and Sugar: 15 grams.

ROASTED SWEET POTATO AND SPINACH BREAKFAST HASH

- Total Time: 45 minutes
- Prep Time: 15 minutes
- Servings: 4

Ingredients:

- 2 medium sweet potatoes, diced 1/2-inch (about 3 cups)
- 2 tablespoons olive oil, divided
- 1 teaspoon smoked paprika
- 1/2 teaspoon garlic powder
- 1/4 teaspoon salt
- 1/8 teaspoon black pepper
- 1 medium onion, diced
- 3 cups fresh spinach, chopped
- 4 eggs
- 2 tablespoons chopped fresh parsley (for garnish)

Instructions:

1. Initiate by setting your oven to preheat at 400°F (200°C) as the first step. Cover a baking sheet with parchment paper as a preparation step.
2. Start by placing the diced sweet potatoes in a large bowl. Then, add one tablespoon of olive oil, smoked paprika, garlic powder, salt, and black pepper. Give everything a good toss to coat the sweet potatoes evenly with the oil and spices.
3. Scatter the seasoned sweet potato cubes in a single, flat layer on the prepared baking sheet. Bake the sweet potatoes for 20-25 minutes, giving them a good flip halfway through. Aim for tender potatoes with a lightly browned exterior.
4. Get that remaining tablespoon of olive oil going in your large skillet over medium heat. Throw in the diced onion and cook, giving it a stir every now and then, until it softens and turns a light brown. This should take about 5-7 minutes.
5. Add the chopped spinach to the skillet with the onion. Add the spinach and cook, tossing often, for 2-3 minutes until wilted.
6. Once the sweet potatoes are fork-tender and beautifully browned, toss them into the skillet with the onions and spinach.
7. Pop a lid on the skillet and turn the heat down to low. Let it cook for 4-6 minutes. This will steam the eggs to your desired doneness. The whites will be firm, and the yolks will be runny for softer eggs or cooked through for a harder yolk.

8. Take the skillet off the heat and give your delicious Roasted Sweet Potato and Spinach Breakfast Hash a sprinkle of chopped fresh parsley for some extra flair!
9. Serve the hash immediately, either directly from the skillet or divided onto plates.

Nutritional breakdown per serving:

Calories: 265 kcal, Protein: 10 grams, Carbohydrates: 32 grams, Fat: 12 grams, Saturated Fat: 2 grams, Cholesterol: 186 milligrams, Sodium: 186 milligrams, Fiber: 6 grams, and Sugar: 8 grams.

MEDITERRANEAN TUNA SALAD STUFFED TOMATOES

- Total Time: 30 minutes
- Prep Time: 20 minutes
- Servings: 6 (as a main dish)

Ingredients:

- Tuna Salad:
- 10 oz flaked tuna (canned)
- 1/4 cup diced cucumber
- 1/4 cup diced red bell pepper
- 2 tablespoons diced red onion
- 2 tablespoons chopped fresh parsley
- 2 tablespoons olive oil
- 1 tablespoon lemon juice
- 1 teaspoon Dijon mustard
- 1/4 teaspoon dried oregano
- 1/4 teaspoon salt
- 1/8 teaspoon black pepper
- Tomato Boats:
- 6 medium tomatoes, halved horizontally
- 2 tablespoons crumbled feta cheese

Instructions:

1. Toss together the flaked tuna with a vibrant mix of chopped ingredients: crisp cucumber, juicy red bell pepper, pungent red onion, and fragrant fresh parsley. They'll create a delightful textural and flavor explosion in every bite!
2. Whip up a zesty dressing in a small bowl. Simply whisk together olive oil, a squeeze of lemon juice, a dollop of Dijon mustard, a pinch of dried oregano, and a dash of salt and pepper.
3. Gently fold the dressing into the tuna mixture, making sure each bite gets a touch of that delicious flavor.
4. Using a small spoon or melon baller, scoop out the seeds and pulp from the center of each tomato half, leaving a shallow well.
5. Arrange the tomato halves, cut-side up, on a serving platter or baking sheet.
6. Divide the tuna salad evenly among the tomato halves, gently pressing it into the wells.

7. Finish the tuna salad with a sprinkle of crumbled feta cheese. The salty bites will add a delightful pop against the creamy mixture.
8. Dig in right away, or store the tuna salad in the refrigerator for a refreshing meal whenever you're ready.

Nutritional breakdown per serving:

Calories (as a main dish, 1 stuffed tomato): 179 kcal, Protein: 15 grams, Carbohydrates: 9 grams, Fat: 10 grams, Saturated Fat: 1 grams, Cholesterol: 24 milligrams, Sodium: 461 milligrams, Fiber: 2 grams, and Sugar: 5 grams.

CHAPTER 3
DINNER RECIPES

GRILLED SALMON WITH ROASTED ASPARAGUS AND LEMON-DILL SAUCE

- Total Time: 40 minutes
- Prep Time: 20 minutes
- Servings: 4

Ingredients:

Salmon:

- 4 (6 oz) salmon fillets, skin-on
- 2 tablespoons olive oil
- 1 teaspoon garlic powder
- 1/2 teaspoon paprika
- 1/4 teaspoon salt
- 1/4 teaspoon black pepper

Asparagus:

- 1 lb trimmed asparagus (cut 2-in)
- 1 tablespoon olive oil
- 1/4 teaspoon salt
- 1/8 teaspoon black pepper
- Lemon-Dill Sauce:
- 1/2 cup plain Greek yogurt
- 2 tablespoons freshly squeezed lemon juice
- 1 tablespoon chopped fresh dill
- 1 teaspoon Dijon mustard
- 1/4 teaspoon garlic powder
- 1/8 teaspoon salt
- 1/8 teaspoon black pepper

Instructions:

1. Get your grill nice and hot! Pre-heat to medium-high, around 400-450°F.
2. Make the lemon-dill sauce:
3. In a small bowl, whisk together the Greek yogurt, lemon juice, chopped dill, Dijon mustard, garlic powder, salt, and black pepper. Set aside.
4. Prepare the salmon:

5. Dry the salmon fillets with paper towels. Then, place them on a plate or in a shallow dish.
6. Give the salmon a drizzle of olive oil (about 2 tablespoons) and a generous sprinkle of garlic powder, paprika, salt, and black pepper. Rub the seasoning evenly over the fillets.

Roast the asparagus:

1. Preheat your oven to 400°F.
2. Lightly coat the asparagus in a flavorful mix. In a medium bowl, toss the asparagus pieces with 1 tablespoon of olive oil, a pinch of salt, and a sprinkle of black pepper.
3. Arrange the seasoned asparagus on a baking sheet in an even layer.
4. Roast the asparagus for 12-15 minutes, or until tender and lightly browned.

Grill the salmon:

1. Get those seasoned salmon fillets sizzling! Place them skin-down on your preheated grill.
2. Grill the salmon for 4-6 minutes per side, or until it flakes easily with a fork and reaches your desired doneness.

Serve the dish:

1. Arrange the grilled salmon fillets on plates or a serving platter.
2. Top each salmon fillet with a generous dollop of the lemon-dill sauce.
3. Serve the roasted asparagus alongside the salmon.

Nutritional breakdown per serving:

Calories: 335 kcal, Protein: 36 grams, Carbohydrates: 8 grams, Fat: 18 grams, Saturated Fat: 3 grams, Cholesterol: 92 milligrams, Sodium: 547 milligrams, Fiber: 3 grams, and Sugar: 3 grams.

QUINOA AND BLACK BEAN STUFFED SWEET POTATOES

- Total Time: 1 hour 10 minutes
- Prep Time: 20 minutes
- Servings: 4

Ingredients:

- 4 medium sweet potatoes, scrubbed clean
- 1 cup cooked quinoa
- 15 oz canned black beans, drained
- 1/2 cup diced red onion
- 1/2 cup diced red bell pepper
- 2 tablespoons chopped fresh cilantro
- 1 tablespoon lime juice
- 1 teaspoon ground cumin
- 1/2 teaspoon garlic powder
- 1/4 teaspoon chili powder
- 1/4 teaspoon salt
- 1/8 teaspoon black pepper
- 1/2 cup shredded cheese
- 2 tablespoons chopped green onions (for garnish)

Instructions:

1. Ahead of baking, set your oven temperature to 400°F (200°C) to ensure it's properly preheated.
2. Prep the sweet potatoes for roasting. Arrange the sweet potato halves directly on the oven rack and bake them for 50-60 minutes, or until a fork can easily pierce through the flesh, indicating they are tender. Allow the sweet potatoes to cool for 5-10 minutes.
3. In a bowl, combine the cooked quinoa, black beans, red onion, and red bell pepper. This forms the base of your salad. Thoroughly mix all the ingredients together to blend the flavors.
4. Split the baked sweet potatoes lengthwise into halves. To create a boat-like shape, use a spoon to scoop out the flesh from the baked sweet potato halves, leaving a 1/4-inch border around the skin. Transfer the scooped-out sweet potato flesh to the bowl with the quinoa and black bean mixture. Mash the sweet potato flesh lightly with a fork to incorporate it into the mixture.

5. Spoon the quinoa and black bean mixture back into the sweet potato "boats," dividing it evenly among the 8 halves.
6. Sprinkle the shredded cheddar cheese (or vegan cheese) over the top of the stuffed sweet potato halves.
7. Place the stuffed sweet potato halves back into the oven and let them bake for an additional 10-15 minutes. Bake until the cheese on top has completely melted and is bubbling.
8. Once the stuffed sweet potatoes have finished baking, take them out of the oven and top them with the chopped green onions as a garnish.
9. Serve hot and enjoy!

Nutritional breakdown per serving:

Calories (1 stuffed sweet potato half): 283 kcal, Protein: 10 grams, Carbohydrates: 48 grams, Fat: 5 grams, Saturated Fat: 3 grams, Cholesterol: 15 milligrams, Sodium: 449 milligrams, Fiber: 8 grams, and Sugar: 11 grams.

CHICKEN FAJITA BOWLS WITH CAULIFLOWER RICE AND GUACAMOLE

- Total Time: 45 minutes
- Prep Time: 20 minutes
- Servings: 4

Ingredients:

<u>Chicken Fajitas:</u>

- 1 lb sliced chicken breasts
- 2 tablespoons olive oil
- 1 teaspoon chili powder
- 1 teaspoon cumin
- 1 teaspoon garlic powder
- 1/2 teaspoon smoked paprika
- 1/4 teaspoon cayenne pepper
- 1/2 teaspoon salt
- 1/4 teaspoon black pepper
- 1 red bell pepper, sliced
- 1 green bell pepper, sliced
- 1 medium onion, sliced
- Cauliflower Rice:
- 1 medium head of cauliflower, riced
- 1 tablespoon olive oil
- 1 garlic clove, minced
- 1/4 teaspoon salt
- 1/8 teaspoon black pepper

Guacamole:

- 2 ripe avocados, diced
- 1 tomato, diced
- 2 tablespoons diced red onion
- 1 tablespoon chopped fresh cilantro
- 1 tablespoon lime juice
- 1/4 teaspoon salt
- 1/8 teaspoon black pepper

Instructions:

1. Adjust your oven's thermostat to 400°F (200°C) in preparation for preheating. Line a baking sheet with parchment paper.
2. In a large bowl, toss chicken slices with olive oil, fajita seasoning, and chili powder (if using).
3. Scatter the prepped peppers and onions across the baking sheet. Place the ingredients in the oven and roast them for 15 minutes, or until they have softened slightly and developed a light browning.
4. Break down the cauliflower florets in a food processor with pulsed motions. Aim for a texture similar to rice. Alternatively, grate the cauliflower using the coarse grater attachment on a box grater. Get a large skillet nice and hot with olive oil over medium heat. Pour in the cauliflower rice and cook, giving it frequent stirs, for 5-7 minutes until tender-crisp. Season with salt and pepper to taste.
5. While the chicken simmers, get another large skillet hot over medium-high heat. Sauté the chicken mixture for 5-7 minutes, stirring periodically, until golden brown and cooked through.
6. Divide the cauliflower rice among bowls. Top each bowl with roasted vegetables, cooked chicken, and a generous dollop of guacamole.
7. In a small bowl, combine mashed avocado, lime juice, red onion, cilantro, diced tomato (if using), salt, and pepper. Mix until well combined.

Nutritional breakdown per serving:

Calories: 365 kcal, Protein: 29 grams, Carbohydrates: 24 grams, Fat: 10 grams, Saturated Fat: 3 grams, Cholesterol: 65 milligrams, Sodium: 579 milligrams, Fiber: 10 grams, and Sugar: 6 grams.

BAKED COD WITH MANGO SALSA AND ROASTED BRUSSELS SPROUTS

- Total Time: 50 minutes
- Prep Time: 25 minutes
- Servings: 4

Ingredients:

Baked Cod:

- 4 (6 oz) cod fillets
- 2 tablespoons olive oil
- 1 teaspoon garlic powder
- 1 teaspoon paprika
- 1/2 teaspoon salt
- 1/4 teaspoon black pepper

Mango Salsa:

- 1 ripe mango, diced
- 1 tomato, diced
- 1/4 cup diced red onion
- 2 tablespoons chopped fresh cilantro
- 1 tablespoon lime juice
- 1/4 teaspoon salt
- 1/8 teaspoon black pepper

Roasted Brussels Sprouts:

- 1 lb Brussels sprouts, trimmed and halved
- 2 tablespoons olive oil
- 1 teaspoon garlic powder
- 1/2 teaspoon salt
- 1/4 teaspoon black pepper

Instructions:

1. Turn your oven on and set it to 200°C (400°F) to preheat. While it warms up, prepare two baking sheets by lining them with parchment paper.

2. Whip up a spice rub in a small bowl by combining olive oil, paprika, garlic powder, salt, and pepper. Dry off any surface moisture on the cod fillets with paper towels. Then, brush them liberally with the prepared spice mixture.
3. In a medium bowl, combine diced mango, red onion, jalapeno (if using), cilantro, lime juice, salt, and pepper. Stir well and set aside.
4. On a prepared baking sheet, toss the Brussels sprouts with olive oil, thyme, salt, and pepper. Make sure they're in a single layer for even roasting.
5. Place both baking sheets with cod and Brussels sprouts in the preheated oven. Bake for 20-25 minutes, or until the cod is flakey and cooked through (internal temperature reaches 145°F) and the Brussels sprouts are tender and slightly browned.
6. Divide the cod fillets among plates. Top each with a generous portion of mango salsa and roasted Brussels sprouts. Enjoy!

Nutritional breakdown per serving:

Calories: 325 kcal, Protein: 33 grams, Carbohydrates: 23 grams, Fat: 13 grams, Saturated Fat: 2 grams, Cholesterol: 65 milligrams, Sodium: 552 milligrams, Fiber: 6 grams, and Sugar: 9 grams.

LENTIL AND VEGETABLE CURRY WITH BASMATI RICE

- Total Time: 60 minutes
- Prep Time: 20 minutes
- Servings: 4

Ingredients:

Lentil and Vegetable Curry:

- 1 cup dried red lentils, rinsed
- 2 cups vegetable broth
- 1 tablespoon olive oil
- 1 onion, diced
- 3 cloves garlic, minced
- 1 tablespoon grated fresh ginger
- 1 tablespoon curry powder
- 1 teaspoon ground cumin
- 1 teaspoon ground coriander
- 1/2 teaspoon ground turmeric
- 1/4 teaspoon cayenne pepper (optional)
- 1 can (14 oz) diced tomatoes
- 2 cups chopped mixed vegetables (such as cauliflower, bell pepper, and spinach)
- 1/2 cup coconut milk
- 1/4 cup chopped fresh cilantro
- Salt and black pepper to taste

Basmati Rice:

- 1 cup basmati rice
- 2 cups water
- 1/2 teaspoon salt

Instructions:

Lentil and Vegetable Curry:

1. Start by adding the rinsed lentils and vegetable broth to a medium saucepan. Bring the ingredients to a boil, then reduce the heat and let the mixture simmer for 15-20 minutes, simmering until the lentils have become tender. Drain off any remaining liquid, if necessary.

2. Position a large skillet or Dutch oven on the stovetop and set the heat to medium. Once the pan is hot, pour in the olive oil. Cook the diced onion in the heated oil, sautéing for 3-4 minutes until the onion pieces become translucent.
3. Introduce the minced garlic and grated ginger into the skillet. Cook the spices for 1 minute, stirring the mixture constantly to prevent burning and allow the aromas to develop.
4. Add the curry powder, cumin, coriander, turmeric, and cayenne pepper (if using) to the skillet. Stir the spices and cook them for 1 minute to toast and activate their flavors.
5. Add the diced tomatoes (with their juices), chopped mixed vegetables, and the cooked lentils. Stir to combine.
6. Stir in the coconut milk and bring everything to a low simmer. Decrease the heat and allow the curry to simmer for 15-20 minutes. The vegetables are done when they're tender enough to be easily pierced with a fork.
7. Take the curry off the heat and stir in the chopped cilantro. Season with salt and black pepper to your preferred taste.

Basmati Rice:

1. In a medium-sized saucepan, mix together the basmati rice, water, and salt. Crank up the heat to high and wait for the contents to come to a full boil.
2. When the mixture comes to a boil, turn down the heat to low in order to sustain a gentle simmering. Securely cover the saucepan with a lid and let the contents simmer for 15-18 minutes. Keep cooking the mixture until the rice becomes tender and all the liquid has been fully absorbed.
3. Gently take the saucepan off the heat and let the rice sit undisturbed, with the lid still on, for 5 minutes.
4. Lightly run a fork through the cooked rice to fluff it up before serving.

Serving:

1. Serve the Lentil and Vegetable Curry over the Basmati Rice.
2. Garnish with additional chopped cilantro, if desired.

Nutritional breakdown per serving:

Calories: 412 kcal, Protein: 16 grams, Carbohydrates: 67 grams, Fat: 10 grams, Saturated Fat: 5 grams, Cholesterol: 0 milligrams, Sodium: 688 milligrams, Fiber: 12 grams, and Sugar: 6 grams.

SUMMERY SKEWERS: SHRIMP, PINEAPPLE, AND BELL PEPPERS ON THE GRILL

- Total Time: 30 minutes
- Prep Time: 15 minutes
- Servings: 4

Ingredients:

- 1 lb large shrimp, peeled and deveined
- 1 fresh pineapple, cut into 1-inch cubes (about 2 cups)
- 2 bell peppers (any color), cut into 1-inch pieces
- 2 tablespoons olive oil
- 2 tablespoons lime juice
- 1 tablespoon honey
- 1 teaspoon garlic powder
- 1 teaspoon smoked paprika
- 1/4 teaspoon cayenne pepper (optional)
- Salt and black pepper to taste
- Wooden or metal skewers

Instructions:

1. Soak wooden skewers 30 minutes to prevent burning on the grill.
2. In a large bowl, combine the shrimp, pineapple cubes, and bell pepper pieces.
3. In a small bowl, create a smoky-sweet marinade by whisking olive oil, lime juice, honey, garlic powder, smoked paprika, and a touch of cayenne pepper (optional). Season with salt and black pepper for a well-rounded flavor.
4. Gently toss the shrimp and vegetables with the marinade to ensure everything is evenly coated. Let the bowl sit covered in the fridge for 30 minutes to 1 hour. The flavors deepen as the ingredients marinate.
5. Fire up the grill or grill pan! Preheat to medium-high heat.
6. Thread the marinated shrimp, pineapple, and bell pepper pieces onto the skewers, alternating the ingredients.
7. Grill the skewers for 2-3 minutes per side, or until the shrimp are opaque and the vegetables are slightly charred.
8. Serve the grilled shrimp skewers immediately, garnished with any remaining marinade, if desired.

Nutritional breakdown per serving:

Calories: 252 kcal, Protein: 24 grams, Carbohydrates: 24 grams, Fat: 8 grams, Saturated Fat: 1 grams, Cholesterol: 172 milligrams, Sodium: 435 milligrams, Fiber: 3 grams, and Sugar: 17 grams.

ROASTED VEGETABLE LASAGNA WITH CASHEW BÉCHAMEL SAUCE

- Total Time: 1 hour 30 minutes
- Prep Time: 30 minutes
- Servings: 8-10

Ingredients:

- 2 cups diced zucchini
- 2 cups diced eggplant
- 1 red bell pepper, diced
- 1 yellow onion, diced
- 2 tablespoons olive oil
- Salt and black pepper to taste
- 1 cup soaked cashews (4 hrs or overnight)
- 2 cups unsweetened almond milk
- 2 tablespoons nutritional yeast
- 1 teaspoon garlic powder
- 1/2 teaspoon onion powder
- 1/4 teaspoon ground nutmeg
- Salt and black pepper to taste
- 9 lasagna noodles (gluten-free, if desired)
- 1 cup grated vegan mozzarella cheese (optional)
- 1/4 cup fresh basil leaves, chopped

Instructions:

Roasted Vegetables:

1. To commence with the recipe, start by preheating your oven to 400°F (200°C).
2. Prep the vegetables: dice zucchini, eggplant, bell pepper, and onion. Toss all the goodies together in a large bowl. Don't forget to add olive oil, salt, and pepper for extra flavor!
3. To ensure even cooking, distribute the vegetables in a single layer across a large parchment-lined baking sheet.
4. Roast the vegetables for 20-25 minutes, giving them a stir halfway through, until they become tender and develop a light browning. Remove from the oven and set aside.

Cashew Béchamel Sauce:

1. Drain and rinse the soaked cashews.

2. In a high-speed blender, combine the soaked cashews, almond milk, nutritional yeast, garlic powder, onion powder, and nutmeg. Blend until smooth and creamy. Finally, season the mixture with salt and black pepper, adjusting the quantities to match your personal flavor preferences.

Lasagna Assembly:

1. To commence with the recipe, start by preheating your oven to 375°F (190°C).
2. Spread 1/2 cup of the Cashew Béchamel Sauce in the bottom of a 9x13-inch baking dish.
3. Arrange 3 lasagna noodles over the sauce, overlapping slightly.
4. Arrange half of the roasted vegetables on top of the noodles, then cover that layer with 1 cup of the Cashew Béchamel Sauce.
5. Repeat the layers of noodles, roasted vegetables, and Cashew Béchamel Sauce.
6. Place the remaining 3 lasagna noodles on top, then cover that with the rest of the Cashew Béchamel Sauce.
7. If using, sprinkle the grated vegan mozzarella cheese over the top.
8. Seal the baking dish with a layer of foil and cook the lasagna for 45-55 minutes, or until it is piping hot and the sauce is bubbling.
9. For a crispier cheese topping, uncover the dish in the last 10 minutes of baking.
10. Before serving, it's recommended to let the lasagna cool for 10-15 minutes.
11. Garnish with the chopped fresh basil.

Nutritional breakdown per serving:

Calories (based on 10 servings): 328 kcal, Protein: 13 grams, Carbohydrates: 35 grams, Fat: 16 grams, Saturated Fat: 2 grams, Cholesterol: 0 milligrams, Sodium: 373 milligrams, Fiber: 7 grams, and Sugar: 7 grams.

BEEF AND BROCCOLI STIR-FRY WITH BROWN RICE NOODLES

- Total Time: 30 minutes
- Prep Time: 15 minutes
- Servings: 4

Ingredients:

- 1 lb thinly sliced flank steak/sirloin
- 2 cups broccoli florets
- 1 red bell pepper, sliced
- 1 cup sliced mushrooms
- 3 cloves garlic, minced
- 1 tablespoon grated fresh ginger
- 2 tablespoons toasted sesame oil
- 2 tablespoons low-sodium soy sauce
- 1 tablespoon rice vinegar
- 1 teaspoon cornstarch
- 8 oz brown rice noodles
- 2 cups low-sodium beef or vegetable broth

Instructions:

1. Whisk together soy sauce, rice vinegar, and cornstarch in a small bowl. Whisk until the cornstarch is dissolved and set aside.
2. Start by boiling a large pot of water. Once boiling, add the brown rice noodles. Cook them for 5-7 minutes, following the package instructions for tenderness. Drain the noodles through a colander and set them aside.
3. Get a large skillet or wok going over high heat. Add the sesame oil and let it heat up. Toss in the sliced beef and stir-fry constantly for 2-3 minutes. You want the beef to be brown around the edges but still have a hint of pink in the center. Take the beef out of the skillet and put it on a plate nearby.
4. Throw the broccoli, bell pepper, and mushrooms into the same skillet. Stir-fry them for 3-4 minutes, aiming for a crisp-tender texture.
5. Finely chop the garlic and ginger. Add the chopped aromatics to the heated skillet. Sauté the aromatic ingredients for approximately 1 minute, stirring frequently, until their fragrance is released and intensified.
6. Return the beef to the skillet and pour in the soy sauce mixture. Continue cooking the mixture in the skillet, stirring frequently, for 1 to 2 minutes. Continue simmering

the contents of the skillet, stirring occasionally, until the sauce has reduced and evenly coats the beef and vegetables.

7. Incorporate the pre-cooked brown rice noodles into the skillet, gently tossing and mixing everything together. Continue cooking just until the noodles are warmed through and thoroughly combined with the sauce.

8. Serve the Beef and Broccoli Stir-Fry with Brown Rice Noodles immediately.

Nutritional breakdown per serving:

Calories: 401 kcal, Protein: 27 grams, Carbohydrates: 43 grams, Fat: 15 grams, Saturated Fat: 3 grams, Cholesterol: 54 milligrams, Sodium: 632 milligrams, Fiber: 4 grams, and Sugar: 3 grams.

BAKED CHICKEN PARMESAN WITH ZUCCHINI NOODLES AND MARINARA

- Total Time: 45 minutes
- Prep Time: 20 minutes
- Servings: 4

Ingredients:

- 4 unbreaded, bone-free chicken breast fillets (approximately 1.5 pounds total)
- 1 cup panko breadcrumbs
- 1/2 cup grated Parmesan cheese
- 1 teaspoon dried oregano
- 1/2 teaspoon garlic powder
- 1/4 teaspoon salt
- 1/4 teaspoon black pepper
- 2 eggs, beaten
- 1 cup marinara sauce
- 1 cup shredded mozzarella cheese
- 3 medium zucchini, spiralized or julienned
- 2 tablespoons olive oil
- 2 cloves garlic, minced
- 1/4 teaspoon salt
- 1/4 teaspoon black pepper
- 1 tablespoon olive oil
- 1 onion, diced
- 3 cloves garlic, minced
- 1 (28 oz) can crushed tomatoes
- 1 teaspoon dried basil
- 1/2 teaspoon dried oregano
- 1/4 teaspoon red pepper flakes (optional)
- Salt and black pepper to taste

Instructions:

Marinara Sauce:

1. Heat a medium saucepan over medium heat. Sauté diced onion in olive oil for 5-7 minutes, until softened and translucent.
2. Add the minced garlic and sauté for 1 minute, until fragrant.

3. Next, stir the crushed tomatoes, dried basil, dried oregano, and red pepper flakes (if using) into the saucepan. Season the contents of the saucepan with salt and black pepper, adjusting the amounts to suit your personal taste preferences.
4. Allow the sauce to come up to a gentle simmer, then let it cook for 15 to 20 minutes, stirring the mixture periodically, until it has thickened to your desired consistency.

Chicken Parmesan:

1. To commence with the recipe, start by preheating your oven to 400°F (200°C).
2. In a shallow bowl, combine the panko breadcrumbs, grated Parmesan cheese, dried oregano, garlic powder, salt, and black pepper.
3. One by one, dip the chicken breasts into the beaten eggs, ensuring the entire surface of each piece is coated. Then, roll the egg-coated chicken in the breadcrumb mixture, covering them completely and evenly.
4. Line a baking sheet with parchment paper. Gently transfer the breadcrumb-encrusted chicken breasts and arrange them in a single, even layer on the parchment-lined baking sheet.
5. Bake the chicken for 20-25 minutes, or until it is thoroughly cooked and the breading turns golden brown.
6. Take the chicken out of the oven and spoon 1/4 cup of marinara sauce over each breast. Place 1/4 cup of shredded mozzarella cheese on top of each serving.
7. To achieve a gloriously melted and bubbly cheese topping, pop the chicken back in the oven for 5-7 more minutes.

Zucchini Noodles:

1. Place a large skillet on the stovetop and heat some olive oil over medium heat.
2. Add the spiralized or julienned zucchini noodles, minced garlic, salt, and black pepper.
3. Cook the zucchini noodles for 3-5 minutes, stirring occasionally, until they are tender but still have some bite.

To Serve:

1. Divide the zucchini noodles among 4 plates.
2. Top each serving of zucchini noodles with a baked Chicken Parmesan breast.
3. Serve the dish with the remaining marinara sauce on the side.

Nutritional breakdown per serving:

Calories: 489 kcal, Protein: 48 grams, Carbohydrates: 33 grams, Fat: 19 grams, Saturated Fat: 6 grams, Cholesterol: 151 milligrams, Sodium: 1039 milligrams, Fiber: 5 grams, and Sugar: 9 grams.

MEDITERRANEAN BAKED COD WITH TOMATOES, OLIVES, AND ARTICHOKES

- Total Time: 45 minutes
- Prep Time: 15 minutes
- Servings: 4

Ingredients:

- 4 (6-oz) cod fillets
- 2 tablespoons olive oil, divided
- 1 pint cherry tomatoes, halved
- 14 oz quartered artichoke hearts (drained)
- 1/2 cup pitted kalamata olives, halved
- 3 cloves garlic, minced
- 1 teaspoon dried oregano
- 1/2 teaspoon dried basil
- 1/4 teaspoon red pepper flakes (optional)
- Salt and black pepper to taste
- 2 tablespoons chopped fresh parsley, for garnish

Instructions:

1. To commence with the recipe, start by preheating your oven to 400°F (200°C).
2. On medium heat, get 1 tablespoon of olive oil shimmering in a large, oven-safe skillet or baking dish. Add the halved cherry tomatoes, quartered artichoke hearts, and halved kalamata olives. Sauté for 3-4 minutes, stirring occasionally, until the tomatoes start to soften.
3. Add the minced garlic, dried oregano, dried basil, and red pepper flakes (if using). Add salt and pepper to your liking. Let the mixture cook for another 1-2 minutes, until the garlic releases its fragrant aroma.
4. Take the vegetable mixture off the heat to prevent overcooking. Transfer it to a plate or bowl to cool slightly. We'll use it later.
5. In the same skillet or baking dish, add the remaining 1 tablespoon of olive oil. Arrange the cod fillets in the skillet or baking dish.
6. Spoon the sautéed vegetable mixture over and around the cod fillets, making sure to distribute the tomatoes, artichokes, and olives evenly.
7. Bake for 18-22 minutes, or until the cod turns opaque and flakes effortlessly with a fork.
8. Fresh parsley time! Take the cod out of the oven and sprinkle it with the chopped parsley.

Nutritional breakdown per serving:

Calories: 276 kcal, Protein: 32 grams, Carbohydrates: 11 grams, Fat: 12 grams, Saturated Fat: 2 grams, Cholesterol: 70 milligrams, Sodium: 704 milligrams, Fiber: 4 grams, and Sugar: 3 grams.

THAI RED CURRY WITH CHICKEN AND BUTTERNUT SQUASH

- Total Time: 45 minutes
- Prep Time: 20 minutes
- Servings: 4

Ingredients:

- 1 pound cubed chicken breasts
- 2 tablespoons coconut oil, divided
- 1 medium butternut squash, cubed
- 1 medium onion, sliced
- 3 cloves garlic, minced
- 1 tablespoon grated fresh ginger
- 2 tablespoons Thai red curry paste
- 1 cup unsweetened coconut milk
- 1 cup low-sodium chicken broth
- 1 tablespoon fish sauce
- 1 tablespoon brown sugar
- 1 cup thinly sliced red bell pepper
- 1 cup chopped green beans
- 1/4 cup chopped fresh cilantro
- Lime wedges for serving

Instructions:

1. Get 1 tablespoon coconut oil shimmering in a large skillet or wok over medium-high heat. Add the cubed chicken and sauté until lightly browned on all sides, about 5-7 minutes. Move the chicken to a plate. We'll come back to it in a bit.
2. Get that leftover coconut oil hot! Heat 1 tablespoon in the pan over medium-high heat. Add the cubed butternut squash and sauté for 5-7 minutes, or until the squash is lightly browned and starting to soften.
3. Sauté the sliced onions in the skillet for 2-3 minutes, until they turn translucent.
4. Add the minced garlic and grated ginger. Sauté for 1 minute, until they release their fragrant aroma.
5. Stir it in to coat the vegetables and cook for 1-2 minutes, stirring constantly. This will awaken the flavors of the curry paste.
6. Pour in the coconut milk and broth, then stir to combine. Add the fish sauce and brown sugar. Bring it all to a simmer.

7. Add the sautéed chicken, sliced red bell pepper, and green beans to the skillet. Reduce the heat to medium-low and simmer for 10-15 minutes, or until the squash is tender and the chicken is cooked through.
8. Stir in the chopped fresh cilantro for a burst of freshness.
9. Serve your Thai Red Curry with Chicken and Butternut Squash right away. Don't forget the lime wedges for a squeeze of fresh citrus on the side.

Nutritional breakdown per serving:

Calories: 380 kcal, Protein: 27 grams, Carbohydrates: 35 grams, Fat: 16 grams, Saturated Fat: 10 grams, Cholesterol: 70 milligrams, Sodium: 560 milligrams, Fiber: 6 grams, and Sugar: 9 grams.

GRILLED PORK TENDERLOIN WITH ROASTED SWEET POTATO AND KALE

- Total Time: 45 minutes
- Prep Time: 20 minutes
- Servings: 4

Ingredients:

- 1 lb trimmed pork tenderloin
- 2 tablespoons olive oil, divided
- 1 teaspoon smoked paprika
- 1 teaspoon garlic powder
- 1 teaspoon dried thyme
- Salt and black pepper to taste
- 2 cups cubed sweet potatoes
- 4 cups chopped kale, stems removed
- 2 tablespoons balsamic vinegar
- 1 tablespoon honey
- 1 tablespoon Dijon mustard
- 2 cloves garlic, minced
- 1/4 cup toasted pine nuts (optional)

Instructions:

1. Preheat your grill or grill pan, whichever you're using, to medium-high heat.
2. In a bowl, whisk together olive oil, smoked paprika, garlic powder, thyme, salt, and pepper. Coat the pork tenderloin generously with the spice rub.
3. Place it on your preheated grill or grill pan. Cook for 12-15 minutes, turning it a few times, until it reaches 145°F (63°C) inside. Transfer the grilled pork tenderloin to a cutting board and let it rest for 5 minutes before slicing.
4. While the pork is grilling, preheat your oven to 400°F (200°C). Get those sweet potatoes roasting! Toss them with the remaining olive oil on a baking sheet. Season and roast (oven temperature) 20-25 minutes, until tender-brown.
5. Whisk balsamic vinegar, honey, Dijon mustard, garlic in a bowl. This flavorful mixture will coat the kale later. Toss the kale mixture until the kale is evenly coated.
6. Slice the grilled pork tenderloin into 1/2-inch thick slices.
7. Divide the roasted sweet potatoes and kale salad evenly among four plates. Top each plate with the sliced pork tenderloin.
8. Don't forget the crunch! Top your salad with the toasted pine nuts.

Nutritional breakdown per serving:

Calories: 350 kcal, Protein: 32 grams, Carbohydrates: 30 grams, Fat: 12 grams, Saturated Fat: 2 grams, Cholesterol: 90 milligrams, Sodium: 330 milligrams, Fiber: 6 grams, and Sugar: 13 grams.

VEGETABLE FRITTATA WITH GOAT CHEESE AND SPINACH

- Total Time: 45 minutes
- Prep Time: 20 minutes
- Servings: 6

Ingredients:

- 8 large eggs
- 1/4 cup unsweetened almond milk
- 1/4 teaspoon salt
- 1/4 teaspoon black pepper
- 2 tablespoons olive oil
- 1 medium zucchini, diced
- 1 medium bell pepper, diced
- 1 cup sliced mushrooms
- 3 cups fresh spinach, chopped
- 4 ounces crumbled goat cheese
- 2 tablespoons chopped fresh basil (optional)

Instructions:

1. To commence with the recipe, start by preheating your oven to 375°F (190°C).
2. In a bowl, whisk together the eggs and almond milk. Season with salt & pepper (to taste). Set aside.
3. In a 10-inch oven-safe nonstick skillet, heat the olive oil over medium heat. Add the diced zucchini, bell pepper, and sliced mushrooms. Sauté the vegetables for 5-7 minutes, or until they are tender and lightly browned.
4. Toss in the spinach and cook 2-3 minutes, wilted and tender.
5. Gently slide the egg mixture over the vegetables in the pan. Swirl the pan gently to distribute the vegetables evenly.
6. For an extra burst of tangy flavor and creamy texture, crumble goat cheese and sprinkle it generously over the top of the frittata before cooking it through.
7. Transfer the skillet to the preheated oven. In 18-20 minutes, your frittata will be transformed - fully set with a lightly golden top that beckons you to dig in.
8. Take the frittata out of the oven and let it sit for 5 minutes.
9. Garnish the frittata with the chopped fresh basil, if using.
10. Cut the frittata into 6 equal slices and serve hot.

Nutritional breakdown per serving:

Calories: 210 kcal, Protein: 15 grams, Carbohydrates: 8 grams, Fat: 14 grams, Saturated Fat: 5 grams, Cholesterol: 275 milligrams, Sodium: 320 milligrams, Fiber: 2 grams, and Sugar: 3 grams.

SALMON BURGERS WITH AVOCADO AND CUCUMBER SLAW

- Total Time: 40 minutes
- Prep Time: 20 minutes
- Servings: 4

Ingredients:

- 1 lb fresh salmon fillets, skin removed and finely chopped
- 1/4 cup panko breadcrumbs
- 2 tablespoons finely chopped fresh dill
- 2 tablespoons Dijon mustard
- 1 tablespoon lemon juice
- 1 teaspoon grated lemon zest
- 1/4 teaspoon salt
- 1/4 teaspoon black pepper
- 1 tablespoon olive oil
- 2 cups thinly sliced cucumber
- 1 avocado, diced
- 1/4 cup plain Greek yogurt
- 2 tablespoons lemon juice
- 1 tablespoon honey
- 1/4 teaspoon salt
- 1/4 teaspoon black pepper
- 2 tablespoons chopped fresh cilantro
- 4 whole wheat hamburger buns, toasted

Instructions:

1. In a large bowl, gently mix together the chopped salmon, panko breadcrumbs, fresh dill, Dijon mustard, lemon juice, lemon zest, salt, and black pepper until well combined.
2. Pat the salmon mixture into four evenly sized burgers, each roughly 4 inches in diameter and 1/2 inch thick.
3. Pan-fry the salmon patties in olive oil until golden brown and cooked through, about 3-4 minutes per side.
4. While the salmon patties are cooking, prepare the avocado and cucumber slaw. In a medium bowl, combine the sliced cucumber, diced avocado, Greek yogurt, lemon juice, honey, salt, and black pepper. Gently toss to coat the ingredients.

5. Stir in the chopped fresh cilantro.
6. To assemble the burgers, place one salmon patty on each toasted whole wheat bun. Spoon a heaping helping of the avocado and cucumber slaw onto each salmon patty.
7. Serve the salmon burgers immediately.

Nutritional breakdown per serving:

Calories: 450 kcal, Protein: 28 grams, Carbohydrates: 36 grams, Fat: 25 grams, Saturated Fat: 4 grams, Cholesterol: 70 milligrams, Sodium: 620 milligrams, Fiber: 6 grams, and Sugar: 6 grams.

CHICKEN AND VEGETABLE STIR-FRY WITH GINGER-GARLIC SAUCE

- Total Time: 30 minutes
- Prep Time: 15 minutes
- Servings: 4

Ingredients:

- 1 pound boneless, skinless chicken breasts, cut into 1-inch pieces
- 2 tablespoons vegetable oil
- 1 red bell pepper, sliced
- 1 cup broccoli florets
- 1 cup sliced mushrooms
- 1 cup sugar snap peas, trimmed
- 2 green onions, sliced
- 2 cloves garlic, minced
- 1 tablespoon freshly grated ginger
- 1/4 cup low-sodium soy sauce
- 2 tablespoons rice vinegar
- 2 tablespoons honey
- 1 tablespoon sesame oil
- 1 teaspoon cornstarch
- 1/4 teaspoon red pepper flakes (optional)
- 4 cups cooked brown rice

Instructions:

1. Prepare the Ginger-Garlic Sauce by whisking all ingredients in a small bowl. Leave it to the side.
2. Fire up a large skillet or wok with vegetable oil over high.
3. Cook the chicken, stirring frequently, for 3-4 minutes until it's golden brown and cooked through. Then, transfer it to a plate and set aside.
4. Add the red bell pepper, broccoli, mushrooms, and sugar snap peas to the hot skillet. Cook the vegetables in the stir-fry for 3-4 minutes, until they are crisp-tender.
5. Add the cooked chicken, green onions, garlic, and ginger to the skillet. Stir-fry for an additional 1-2 minutes, or until the garlic and ginger are fragrant.
6. Pour the Ginger-Garlic Sauce into the skillet and bring to a simmer. Cook for 1-2 minutes, or until the sauce has thickened slightly.
7. Serve the Chicken and Vegetable Stir-Fry immediately over the cooked brown rice.

Nutritional breakdown per serving:

Calories: 400 kcal, Protein: 34 grams, Carbohydrates: 43 grams, Fat: 12 grams, Saturated Fat: 2 grams, Cholesterol: 80 milligrams, Sodium: 650 milligrams, Fiber: 5 grams, and Sugar: 10 grams.

BAKED EGGPLANT PARMESAN WITH MARINARA AND BASIL

- Total Time: 1 hour 15 minutes
- Prep Time: 30 minutes
- Servings: 6

Ingredients:

- 2 medium eggplants, sliced into 1/4-inch thick rounds
- 1/2 cup all-purpose flour
- 2 large eggs, beaten
- 1 cup panko breadcrumbs
- 1/2 cup grated Parmesan cheese
- 1 teaspoon dried oregano
- 1/2 teaspoon garlic powder
- 1/4 teaspoon salt
- 1/4 teaspoon black pepper
- 1 tablespoon olive oil
- 1 onion, diced
- 3 cloves garlic, minced
- 1 (28 oz) can crushed tomatoes
- 1 teaspoon dried basil
- 1/2 teaspoon dried oregano
- 1/4 teaspoon red pepper flakes (optional)
- Salt and black pepper to taste
- 1 cup shredded part-skim mozzarella cheese
- 1/4 cup grated Parmesan cheese
- 1/4 cup fresh basil, thinly sliced

Instructions:

1. To commence with the recipe, start by preheating your oven to 375°F (190°C). Line two baking sheets with parchment paper.
2. In a shallow dish, place the flour. In a second shallow dish, beat the eggs. In a third shallow dish, combine the panko breadcrumbs, 1/2 cup Parmesan cheese, oregano, garlic powder, salt, and black pepper.
3. Prepare your breading station with bowls of flour, beaten eggs, and breadcrumbs. Dip the eggplant slices in flour, then the eggs, and finally the breadcrumbs, pressing gently to coat.

4. Arrange the breaded eggplant in a single layer on the baking sheets. Bake them for 15-20 minutes, flipping once during baking. Aim for a beautiful golden brown color and a crispy exterior.
5. While the eggplant is baking, prepare the marinara sauce. Get some olive oil going in a medium saucepan over medium heat. Sauté the onion in olive oil over medium heat for 5 minutes, until translucent. Next, throw in the garlic and cook for just a minute longer.
6. Combine crushed tomatoes, dried herbs, and optional red pepper flakes in the pan. Season with salt and pepper to taste. Simmer gently for 10 minutes, stirring every now and then, to develop the depth of flavor.
7. Start by creating a base layer of marinara sauce in your 9x13 inch baking dish. Spread it out evenly in a thin coat. Arrange the baked eggplant slices in a single layer. Pour the remaining marinara sauce over the first layer. Then, sprinkle with shredded mozzarella and top with 1/4 cup grated Parmesan cheese.
8. Bake uncovered for 25-30 minutes, looking for melted and bubbly cheese. Remove from the oven and sprinkle with the fresh basil.
9. Let the Baked Eggplant Parmesan cool for 5-10 minutes before serving.

Nutritional breakdown per serving:

Calories: 345 kcal, Protein: 19 grams, Carbohydrates: 39 grams, Fat: 14 grams, Saturated Fat: 6grams, Cholesterol: 85 milligrams, Sodium: 650 milligrams, Fiber: 8 grams, and Sugar: 8 grams.

BEEF AND BROCCOLI STUFFED PORTOBELLO MUSHROOMS

- Total Time: 50 minutes
- Prep Time: 20 minutes
- Servings: 4

Ingredients:

- 4 large portobello mushrooms, prepped with stems removed and finely chopped
- 1 tablespoon olive oil
- 1 lb ground beef
- 2 cloves garlic, minced
- 1 teaspoon grated fresh ginger
- 2 cups broccoli florets, finely chopped
- 1/4 cup low-sodium soy sauce
- 2 tablespoons rice vinegar
- 1 tablespoon brown sugar
- 1 teaspoon sesame oil
- 1/4 teaspoon red pepper flakes (optional)
- Salt and black pepper to taste
- 1 cup shredded mozzarella cheese

Instructions:

1. To commence with the recipe, start by preheating your oven to 400°F (200°C). Line a baking sheet with parchment paper.
2. Gently scoop out the stems from the portobello mushroom caps, leaving a 1/2-inch thick shell. Finely chop the removed stems.
3. Get a large skillet going with olive oil over medium-high heat. Add the ground beef and the chopped mushroom stems. Crumble the ground beef with a spatula in the skillet as it cooks. Continue for 5-7 minutes, until the beef is browned and the mushroom stems are tender.
4. After the beef and mushrooms are browned, stir in the garlic and ginger. Let them cook for 1 minute to become fragrant.
5. Stir in the chopped broccoli florets, soy sauce, rice vinegar, brown sugar, and sesame oil. Add a kick of red pepper flakes (optional), along with salt and black pepper, to the pan. Sauté the broccoli for 3-4 minutes, stirring occasionally, until it's crisp-tender.
6. Arrange the portobello mushroom caps, stem-side up, on the prepared baking sheet. Spoon the beef and broccoli mixture evenly into the mushroom caps.
7. Top each stuffed mushroom with shredded mozzarella cheese.

8. Bake for 20-25 minutes, or until the mushrooms are nice and tender and the cheese is melted and bubbly on top.
9. Remove the Beef and Broccoli Stuffed Portobello Mushrooms from the oven and let them cool for 5 minutes before serving.

Nutritional breakdown per serving:

Calories: 350 kcal, Protein: 32 grams, Carbohydrates: 16 grams, Fat: 18 grams, Saturated Fat: 7 grams, Cholesterol: 70 milligrams, Sodium: 620 milligrams, Fiber: 4 grams, and Sugar: 6 grams.

GRILLED SHRIMP SKEWERS WITH PINEAPPLE SALSA

- Total Time: 40 minutes
- Prep Time: 20 minutes
- Servings: 4 (2 skewers per serving)

Ingredients:

- 1 lb large shrimp, peeled and deveined
- 2 tablespoons olive oil
- 2 tablespoons lime juice
- 1 teaspoon garlic powder
- 1 teaspoon chili powder
- 1/2 teaspoon salt
- 8 soaked 6-inch wooden skewers
- 1 cup diced fresh pineapple
- 1/2 cup diced red onion
- 1/4 cup chopped fresh cilantro
- 2 tablespoons lime juice
- 1 jalapeño, seeded and finely chopped (optional)
- 1/4 teaspoon salt

Instructions:

1. In a medium bowl, combine the shrimp, olive oil, lime juice, garlic powder, chili powder, and salt. Toss to coat the shrimp evenly. Cover and refrigerate for 15-20 minutes.
2. As the shrimp marinates, whip up a refreshing pineapple salsa. In a small bowl, toss together diced pineapple, red onion, chopped cilantro, lime juice, jalapeño (optional), and a pinch of salt. Cover and chill until serving.
3. Fire up your grill or grill pan! Aim for medium-high heat.
4. Thread the marinated shrimp onto the soaked skewers. Don't crowd them - leave a little gap between each shrimp for even cooking.
5. Cook the shrimp skewers on the preheated grill for 2-3 minutes per side. Look for the shrimp to turn opaque, which means they're cooked through.
6. Remove the grilled shrimp skewers from the grill and transfer them to a serving platter.
7. Serve the Grilled Shrimp Skewers with the chilled pineapple salsa on the side.

Nutritional breakdown per serving (2 skewers with 1/4 cup salsa):

Calories: 200 kcal, Protein: 21 grams, Carbohydrates: 14 grams, Fat: 8 grams, Saturated Fat: 1 grams, Cholesterol: 170 milligrams, Sodium: 480 milligrams, Fiber: 2 grams, and Sugar: 10 grams.

CHICKEN AND VEGETABLE QUINOA BOWLS WITH TAHINI DRESSING

- Total Time: 45 minutes
- Prep Time: 25 minutes
- Servings: 4

Ingredients:

- 1 cup uncooked quinoa, rinsed
- 2 cups low-sodium chicken or vegetable broth
- 1 lb boneless, skinless chicken breasts, cubed
- 1 tablespoon olive oil
- 1 teaspoon garlic powder
- 1/2 teaspoon paprika
- Salt and black pepper, to taste
- 1 cup broccoli florets
- 1 cup diced sweet potato
- 1 cup sliced zucchini
- 1/4 cup sliced green onions
- 1/4 cup tahini paste
- 2 tablespoons lemon juice
- 2 tablespoons water
- 1 tablespoon honey
- 1 garlic clove, minced
- 1/4 teaspoon ground cumin
- Salt and black pepper, to taste

Instructions:

1. For the quinoa, give it a good rinse first. Next, in a medium saucepan, mix it with chicken or vegetable broth. Simmer the quinoa: Bring the quinoa and broth to a boil, then reduce heat to low, cover, and simmer for 15-20 minutes. You'll know it's done when the quinoa is tender and all the liquid is absorbed. Fluff with a fork and set aside.
2. In a bowl, coat the cubed chicken with olive oil, garlic powder, paprika, salt, and pepper. Toss everything until the chicken is well-seasoned.
3. Heat a large skillet over medium-high heat. Add the seasoned chicken and cook, stirring occasionally, for 6-8 minutes, or until the chicken is cooked through and lightly browned.

4. While the chicken cooks, steam your broccoli florets, diced sweet potato, and sliced zucchini in a steamer basket for 5-7 minutes. Aim for tender vegetables.
5. For the tahini dressing, combine tahini paste, lemon juice, water, honey, garlic, cumin, salt, and pepper in a small bowl. Whisk it all together until smooth and creamy.
6. To assemble the bowls, divide the cooked quinoa among 4 serving bowls. Top each bowl with the cooked chicken, steamed vegetables, and sliced green onions. Drizzle the tahini dressing over the top.

Nutritional breakdown per serving:

Calories: 445 kcal, Protein: 38 grams, Carbohydrates: 44 grams, Fat: 15 grams, Saturated Fat: 2 grams, Cholesterol: 65 milligrams, Sodium: 300 milligrams, Fiber: 7 grams, and Sugar: 8 grams.

BAKED COD WITH ROASTED PEPPERS AND OLIVE TAPENADE

- Total Cooking Time: 35 minutes
- Prep Time: 15 minutes
- Servings: 4

Ingredients:

- 4 cod fillets (around 6 oz each)
- 1 tbsp olive oil
- 1 tsp dried oregano
- 1/2 tsp garlic powder
- Salt & pepper to taste
- 2 red bell peppers
- 1 yellow bell pepper
- 1 tbsp olive oil
- 1/2 tsp dried thyme
- Salt & pepper to taste
- 1/2 cup pitted Kalamata olives, chopped
- 2 tbsp capers, drained and rinsed
- 2 tbsp fresh parsley leaves, chopped
- 1 tbsp lemon juice
- 2 cloves garlic, minced
- 2 tbsp olive oil

Instructions:

1. To commence with the recipe, start by preheating your oven to 400°F (200°C). Line a baking sheet with parchment paper.
2. Wash and halve the bell peppers, removing the seeds and membranes. Slice them into thick strips. In a large bowl, toss the pepper strips with olive oil, thyme, salt, and pepper. Spread the seasoned peppers on the prepared baking sheet.
3. Pop the baking sheet with peppers into your preheated oven. Roast them for 20-25 minutes, or until they're softened up and have some nice char around the edges.
4. Dry the fillets with paper towels. Next, whip up a spice rub in a small bowl by mixing olive oil, oregano, garlic powder, salt, and pepper. Rub this delicious mixture generously onto both sides of the cod to coat them evenly.
5. Once the peppers are roasted, remove the baking sheet from the oven. Arrange the fillets in a single layer on top. Continue baking for 10-12 minutes, returning the

baking sheet to the oven. Aim for cooked-through cod - opaque and flaking easily with a fork.

6. While the cod bakes, prepare the tapenade. In a food processor, combine chopped olives, capers, parsley, lemon juice, garlic, and olive oil. Pulse until a chunky paste forms. Drizzle in more olive oil for a looser consistency.

7. Divide the roasted peppers and cod fillets among plates. Top each serving with a generous dollop of olive tapenade. Enjoy!

Nutritional breakdown per serving:

Calories: 280 kcal, Protein: 29 grams, Carbohydrates: 8 grams, Fat: 15 grams, Saturated Fat: 2 grams, Cholesterol: 65 milligrams, Sodium: 590 milligrams, Fiber: 2 grams, and Sugar: 3 grams.

HEARTY BUTTERNUT SQUASH AND CHICKPEA CURRY WITH BASMATI RICE

- Total Cooking Time: 50 minutes
- Prep Time: 15 minutes
- Servings: 4

Ingredients:

- 1 tablespoon olive oil
- 1 medium onion, chopped
- 2 cloves garlic, minced
- 1 inch ginger, grated
- 1 tablespoon curry powder
- 1/2 teaspoon turmeric
- 1/2 teaspoon ground cumin
- 1/4 teaspoon chili powder (optional, for more heat)
- 1 (13.5 oz) can coconut milk
- 1 (14.5 oz) can diced tomatoes, undrained
- 1 cup vegetable broth
- 2 lbs butternut squash, peeled, seeded, cubed
- 15-oz can of rinsed chickpeas
- 1/2 cup chopped fresh cilantro
- Salt & pepper to taste
- 1 cup basmati rice, rinsed
- 1 1/2 cups water
- 1/4 teaspoon salt

Instructions:

1. In a medium saucepan, combine rinsed basmati rice, water, and salt. Crank up the heat to high and bring the contents of the pot to a vigorous boil. Once it's at a full boil, dial down the heat to low, cover the pot with a tightly fitting lid, and let it simmer for 18 to 20 minutes, or until the rice has fully cooked through and reached a fluffy consistency. Take the pot off the heat and keep it covered for 5 more minutes. Then, use a fork to fluff and separate the cooked rice.
2. Meanwhile, heat some olive oil in a large pot or Dutch oven over medium heat. Sauté the chopped onion until softened and translucent, about 5 minutes. Next, stir in the minced garlic and grated ginger. Cook the garlic and ginger for approximately 1 minute, or until their aroma begins to fill the air.

3. Add the curry powder, turmeric, cumin, and chili powder (if using) to the pot. Sauté the spices for 30 seconds, stirring continuously, to help draw out their aromatic oils and flavors.
4. Add the coconut milk, diced tomatoes along with their juices, and the vegetable broth to the pot. Stir everything together and let the mixture come up to a gentle simmer.
5. Add the cubed butternut squash to the simmering curry sauce. Cover the pot partially, leaving a small gap in the lid, and let the mixture continue simmering for 15-20 minutes, or until the butternut squash cubes become tender yet still maintain a slight firmness.
6. Stir the drained and rinsed chickpeas and freshly chopped cilantro into the simmering mixture. Season the dish with salt and pepper, adjusting the amounts to your personal taste preferences. Allow the dish to continue simmering for 5 more minutes, letting the flavors meld together.
7. Divide the cooked basmati rice among serving bowls. Top each bowl with a generous portion of the butternut squash and chickpea curry. Enjoy!

Nutritional breakdown per serving:

Calories: 435 kcal, Protein: 12 grams, Carbohydrates: 63 grams, Fat: 16 grams, Saturated Fat: 8 grams, Cholesterol: 0 milligrams, Sodium: 615 milligrams, Fiber: 9 grams, and Sugar: 6 grams.

GRILLED CHICKEN AND PEACH SALAD WITH BALSAMIC GLAZE

- Total Cooking Time: 35 minutes
- Prep Time: 15 minutes
- Servings: 4

Ingredients:

- 1 pound of boneless, skinless chicken breasts (approximately 2 breasts)
- 2 tablespoons olive oil
- 1 tablespoon dried oregano
- 1/2 teaspoon garlic powder
- 1/2 teaspoon paprika
- Salt & pepper to taste
- 4 cups of mixed greens, such as spring mix, arugula, or baby spinach
- 2 ripe peaches, pitted and sliced
- 1/2 cup crumbled feta cheese
- 1/4 cup chopped red onion
- 1/4 cup chopped fresh basil leaves
- 1/4 cup balsamic vinegar
- 2 tablespoons brown sugar
- 1 tablespoon Dijon mustard

Instructions:

1. In a large bowl, combine olive oil, oregano, garlic powder, paprika, salt, and pepper. Add the chicken breasts and gently toss them to ensure even coating. Cover the bowl and refrigerate the chicken for at least 30 minutes, or up to 2 hours for a more intensified flavor.
2. In a small pot, mix together balsamic vinegar, brown sugar, and Dijon mustard. Whisk the ingredients until combined, then heat over medium until simmering. Simmer the mixture for 5-7 minutes, stirring intermittently, until the glaze has slightly thickened. Remove from heat and set aside.
3. Preheat your grill to medium-high heat. If using a gas grill, preheat for 10 minutes with the lid closed. Lightly grease the grill grates to discourage the food from adhering.
4. Take the chicken breasts out of the marinade and dispose of the remaining marinade. Grill the chicken for 5-7 minutes on each side, or until the internal temperature reaches 165°F (74°C) and the meat is fully cooked through.

5. While the chicken grills, arrange the mixed greens on a large serving platter or individual plates. Top with sliced peaches, crumbled feta cheese, chopped red onion, and fresh basil leaves.
6. Once the chicken has finished cooking on the grill, transfer it to a cutting board and let it sit for a few minutes. Afterwards, slice the chicken breasts into strips or bite-sized pieces.
7. Place the sliced grilled chicken pieces on top of the salad. Drizzle the balsamic glaze generously over the salad and chicken. Enjoy!

Nutritional breakdown per serving:

Calories: 339 kcal, Protein: 32 grams, Carbohydrates: 30 grams, Fat: 12 grams, Saturated Fat: 3 grams, Cholesterol: 90 milligrams, Sodium: 421 milligrams, Fiber: 5 grams, and Sugar: 22 grams.

ROASTED VEGETABLE AND FETA STUFFED PORTOBELLO MUSHROOMS

- Total Time: 50 minutes
- Prep Time: 20 minutes
- Servings: 4

Ingredients:

- 4 large portobello mushroom caps with the stems removed and chopped
- 2 tablespoons olive oil, divided
- 1 red bell pepper, diced
- 1 zucchini, diced
- 1 onion, diced
- 3 cloves garlic, minced
- 1 cup crumbled feta cheese
- 2 tablespoons chopped fresh basil
- Salt and pepper to taste

Directions:

1. To commence with the recipe, start by preheating your oven to 400°F (200°C). Line a baking sheet with parchment paper.
2. Add the chopped portobello mushroom caps to a large bowl, then drizzle 1 tablespoon of olive oil over them and toss to coat. Arrange the mushroom caps, gill-side up, on a prepared baking sheet.
3. In a skillet, heat the remaining 1 tablespoon of olive oil over medium heat. Add the chopped mushroom stems, bell pepper, zucchini, onion, and garlic. Sauté until the vegetables are tender, about 8-10 minutes.
4. Once removed from the heat, stir the feta cheese and fresh basil into the contents of the skillet. Flavor the dish with salt and pepper to suit your individual taste.
5. Spoon the vegetable-feta mixture into the mushroom caps, dividing it evenly.
6. Put the stuffed mushrooms in the preheated oven and let them bake for 20-25 minutes, or until the mushrooms are soft and the filling is hot and bubbling.
7. Serve the roasted vegetable and feta stuffed portobello mushrooms immediately.

Nutritional breakdown per serving:

Calories: 180 kcal, Protein: 9 grams, Carbohydrates: 12 grams, Fat: 12 grams, Saturated Fat: 5 grams, Cholesterol: 25 milligrams, Sodium: 370 milligrams, Fiber: 3 grams, and Sugar: 6 grams.

SALMON BURGERS WITH AVOCADO AND CUCUMBER RELISH

- Total Time: 40 minutes
- Prep Time: 20 minutes
- Servings: 4

Ingredients:

- 1 lb fresh salmon, finely chopped or pulsed in a food processor
- 1 egg, lightly beaten
- 1/4 cup panko breadcrumbs
- 2 tablespoons chopped fresh dill
- 1 tablespoon Dijon mustard
- 1 teaspoon lemon zest
- Salt and pepper to taste
- 1 tablespoon olive oil for cooking
- 1 avocado, diced
- 1 cucumber, diced
- 1/4 cup diced red onion
- 2 tablespoons chopped fresh cilantro
- 1 tablespoon lime juice
- Salt and pepper to taste
- 4 whole wheat burger buns
- Lettuce leaves (optional)

Directions:

1. In a bowl, combine the chopped salmon, egg, panko, dill, Dijon mustard, and lemon zest. Season with salt and pepper to taste. Mix well until fully incorporated.
2. Separate the salmon mixture into 4 equal parts and form them into patties.
3. Set a large skillet over medium heat and add the olive oil. Sauté the salmon burgers for 3-4 minutes on each side, or until they are lightly browned and fully cooked.
4. As the burgers cook, prepare the avocado and cucumber relish. In a small bowl, mix together the diced avocado, cucumber, red onion, cilantro, and lime juice. Season with salt and pepper to taste.
5. Serve the salmon burgers on the whole wheat buns, topped with the avocado and cucumber relish and lettuce leaves, if desired.

Nutritional breakdown per serving:

Calories: 390 kcal, Protein: 28 grams, Carbohydrates: 28 grams, Fat: 20 grams, Saturated Fat: 3.5 grams, Cholesterol: 90 milligrams, Sodium: 570 milligrams, Fiber: 6 grams, and Sugar: 4 grams.

LENTIL AND SWEET POTATO SHEPHERD'S PIE

- Total Time: 1 hour 15 minutes
- Prep Time: 30 minutes
- Servings: 6

Ingredients:

- 1 tablespoon olive oil
- 1 onion, diced
- 3 cloves garlic, minced
- 2 carrots, diced
- 2 celery stalks, diced
- 1 cup brown lentils, rinsed
- 1 (15 oz) can diced tomatoes
- 2 cups vegetable broth
- 1 teaspoon dried thyme
- 1 teaspoon dried rosemary
- Salt and pepper to taste
- 3 medium sweet potatoes, peeled and cubed
- 2 tablespoons unsalted butter
- 1/4 cup milk
- Salt and pepper to taste

Instructions:

1. To commence with the recipe, start by preheating your oven to 375°F (190°C).
2. Place a large skillet on the stovetop and set the heat to medium. Pour the olive oil into the preheated skillet. Cook the onion in the skillet for 5 minutes, stirring occasionally, until it becomes translucent.
3. Place the garlic, carrots, and celery into the skillet and sauté them for 3-4 minutes, giving the mixture an occasional stir.
4. Add the lentils, diced tomatoes, vegetable broth, thyme, and rosemary to the skillet. Season with salt and pepper. Turn up the heat to high and allow the mixture to come to a boil. Next, reduce the heat and let the mixture gently simmer for 20-25 minutes, or until the lentils become tender.
5. While the lentil mixture is simmering, prepare the sweet potato topping. Bring the pot of water with the sweet potato cubes to a boil over high heat. Reduce the heat to medium once the water reaches a boil, and let the sweet potato cubes simmer for 15-20 minutes, or until they can be easily pierced with a fork, indicating they have become tender.

6. Drain the cooked sweet potatoes and then mash them together with the butter and milk. Season with salt and pepper to taste.
7. Transfer the lentil filling into a 9x13 inch baking dish. Then, spread the mashed sweet potatoes in an even layer over the top.
8. Put the prepared shepherd's pie in the preheated oven and let it bake for 30-35 minutes, or until the topping develops a golden brown hue.
9. Remove from the oven and let it cool for 10 minutes before serving.

Nutritional breakdown per serving:

Calories: 290 kcal, Protein: 12 grams, Carbohydrates: 44 grams, Fat: 8 grams, Saturated Fat: 3 grams, Cholesterol: 10 milligrams, Sodium: 440 milligrams, Fiber: 10 grams, and Sugar: 9 grams.

CHICKEN FAJITA LETTUCE WRAPS WITH GUACAMOLE

- Total Time: 30 minutes
- Prep Time: 15 minutes
- Servings: 4

Ingredients:

- 1 lb sliced chicken breasts
- 1 tablespoon olive oil
- 1 red bell pepper, sliced
- 1 yellow onion, sliced
- 2 cloves garlic, minced
- 1 tablespoon fajita seasoning
- Salt and pepper to taste
- 2 avocados, diced
- 1/4 cup diced red onion
- 2 tablespoons chopped fresh cilantro
- 1 tablespoon lime juice
- 1/2 teaspoon salt
- 8-10 large lettuce leaves (such as romaine or butter lettuce)

Instructions:

1. Place a large skillet over medium-high heat and allow the olive oil to warm up. Then, add the sliced chicken, bell pepper, onion, and garlic. Simmer the mixture for another 5-7 minutes, stirring occasionally, until the chicken cooks through completely and the vegetables become tender-crisp.
2. Evenly sprinkle the fajita seasoning over the chicken and vegetable blend in the skillet, then stir the mixture until the seasoning is fully incorporated throughout. Add salt and pepper to taste. Once seasoned, remove the skillet from the heat.
3. Place the diced avocados, red onion, cilantro, lime juice, and a small amount of salt in a medium-sized bowl, then mix the ingredients together. Use a fork to mash the ingredients together, but leave some small chunks of avocado intact.
4. To serve, place a spoonful of the chicken fajita filling into each lettuce leaf. Top with a generous amount of the guacamole.
5. Serve the chicken fajita lettuce wraps immediately.

Nutritional breakdown per serving (1 lettuce wrap with 1/4 of the filling and guacamole):

Calories: 260 kcal, Protein: 23 grams, Carbohydrates: 12 grams, Fat: 14 grams, Saturated Fat: 2.5 grams, Cholesterol: 65 milligrams, Sodium: 470 milligrams, Fiber: 7 grams, and Sugar: 4 grams.

BAKED EGGPLANT PARMESAN WITH ZUCCHINI NOODLES

- Total Time: 1 hour 15 minutes
- Prep Time: 30 minutes
- Servings: 4

Ingredients:

- 2 medium eggplants, sliced into 1/4-inch thick rounds
- 1 cup all-purpose flour
- 2 eggs, beaten
- 1 1/2 cups Italian breadcrumbs
- 1 cup grated Parmesan cheese, divided
- 1 jar (24 oz) marinara sauce
- 1 cup shredded mozzarella cheese
- 3 medium zucchinis, spiralized or julienned
- 1 tablespoon olive oil
- 2 cloves garlic, minced
- Salt and pepper to taste

Instructions:

Eggplant Parmesan:

1. To commence with the recipe, start by preheating your oven to 375°F (190°C). Line a baking sheet with parchment paper.
2. Prepare three separate shallow dishes - one with flour, one with beaten eggs, and one with the breadcrumbs combined with 1/2 cup of grated Parmesan cheese.
3. Take the eggplant slices and dip them first in the flour, then in the beaten eggs, and finally coat them thoroughly in the breadcrumb and Parmesan mixture, pressing lightly to help the coating stick.
4. Place the breaded eggplant slices in a single, even layer on the baking sheet that has been prepared.
5. Bake the breaded eggplant slices for 20-25 minutes, flipping them over halfway through the cooking time, until they have turned golden brown and become crispy.
6. Line a 9x13 inch baking dish with a thin layer of marinara sauce. Place the baked eggplant slices in a single, even layer on top of the marinara sauce in the baking dish. Then, pour the remaining marinara sauce over the eggplant and sprinkle the mozzarella cheese on top.
7. Bake for an additional 20-25 minutes, or until the cheese is melted and bubbly.

<u>Zucchini Noodles:</u>

1. Get your large skillet going with some olive oil over medium heat. Once the oil shimmers, toss in the minced garlic and cook until it smells good, roughly a minute.
2. Throw in your spiralized (or julienned) zucchini noodles and toss them with the garlic oil. Cook for 2-3 minutes, aiming for tender-crisp noodles.
3. Give the zucchini noodles some love with salt and pepper.
4. Serve the baked eggplant parmesan over the zucchini noodles, garnished with the remaining 1/2 cup of Parmesan cheese.

Nutritional breakdown per serving:

Calories: 420 kcal, Protein: 26 grams, Carbohydrates: 42 grams, Fat: 18 grams, Saturated Fat: 7 grams, Cholesterol: 115 milligrams, Sodium: 930 milligrams, Fiber: 10 grams, and Sugar: 8 grams.

GRILLED PORK TENDERLOIN WITH ROASTED BROCCOLI AND QUINOA

- Total Cooking Time: 50 minutes
- Prep Time: 15 minutes
- Servings: 4

Ingredients:

- 1 lb pork tenderloin
- 2 tablespoons olive oil
- 1 tablespoon dried thyme
- 1/2 teaspoon garlic powder
- 1/2 teaspoon smoked paprika
- 1/4 teaspoon salt
- 1/4 teaspoon freshly ground black pepper
- 1 head of broccoli, cut into florets
- 1 tablespoon olive oil
- 1/2 teaspoon dried oregano
- 1/4 teaspoon salt
- 1/4 teaspoon freshly ground black pepper
- 1 cup quinoa, rinsed
- 1 3/4 cups water or chicken broth
- 1/4 teaspoon salt

Instructions:

1. In a small bowl, combine olive oil, thyme, garlic powder, smoked paprika, salt, and pepper. Use paper towels to thoroughly pat the pork tenderloin dry. Then, place the pork in a shallow dish or resealable plastic bag and pour the prepared marinade over it. Marinate for at least 30 minutes, or up to 2 hours for deeper flavor.
2. Preheat your grill to medium-high heat. If using a gas grill, preheat for 10 minutes with the lid closed. Lightly coat the grill grates with a thin layer of oil to help prevent the food from sticking.
3. While the pork marinates, cook the quinoa. In a medium saucepan, combine rinsed quinoa, water or chicken broth, and salt. Increase heat to boiling. Reduce heat to low, cover the pot securely, and simmer for 15-20 minutes, or until the quinoa is tender and fluffy. Take the pot off the heat and fluff with a fork. Set aside. Once cooked, take the pot off the heat. With a fork, gently loosen the quinoa, separating the cooked grains. Set aside.

4. Dress the broccoli florets in a large bowl with olive oil, oregano, salt, and pepper.
5. Get your oven heating up to (temperature) and line a baking sheet with parchment paper. Spread the seasoned broccoli florets on the baking sheet in a single layer. Place the baking sheet on a preheated oven rack set to 400°F (200°C). Roast for 15-20 minutes, or until the broccoli is tender-crisp and slightly browned.
6. Take the pork tenderloin out of the marinade and discard the marinade. Grill it for 15-20 minutes, flipping it from time to time, until cooked through. For safe consumption, cook the pork until its internal temperature reaches 145°F (63°C).
7. Divide the cooked quinoa among serving plates. Top each plate with roasted broccoli and sliced pork tenderloin. Enjoy!

Nutritional breakdown per serving:

Calories: 412 kcal, Protein: 36 grams, Carbohydrates: 32 grams, Fat: 16 grams, Saturated Fat: 3 grams, Cholesterol: 80 milligrams, Sodium: 330 milligrams, Fiber: 5 grams, and Sugar: 2 grams.

VEGETABLE AND TOFU STIR-FRY WITH BROWN RICE NOODLES

- Total Cooking Time: 45 minutes
- Prep Time: 20 minutes
- Servings: 4

Ingredients:

Stir-Fry:

- 1 block (14 oz) firm tofu, cubed
- 2 tbsp sesame oil
- 2 cloves garlic, minced
- 1 inch fresh ginger, grated
- 1 red bell pepper, sliced
- 1 cup broccoli florets
- 1 cup sliced mushrooms
- 1 cup snap peas or snow peas
- 2 tbsp low-sodium soy sauce
- 1 tbsp rice vinegar
- 1 tsp sesame seeds (optional)
- 8 oz brown rice noodles
- 2 cups low-sodium vegetable broth
- 2 tbsp low-sodium soy sauce
- 1 tbsp rice vinegar
- 1 tbsp honey
- 1 tsp cornstarch

Directions:

Brown Rice Noodles:

1. Get a large pot going and bring the vegetable broth to a boil.
2. For perfect texture, cook the brown rice noodles according to the package (usually 5-7 minutes).
3. Drain the noodles and set aside.

Stir-Fry:

1. Press the cubed tofu between paper towels to remove excess moisture.

2. Saute the garlic and ginger in the skillet. Cook for 1 minute, stirring frequently, to release their fragrance.
3. Add the pressed tofu cubes and cook for 3-4 minutes per side, until lightly browned. Transfer the tofu to a plate.
4. Add the sliced bell pepper, broccoli florets, mushrooms, and snap peas. Cook the vegetables in the stir-fry for 5-7 minutes, until they reach a tender-crisp doneness.
5. Add the sliced bell pepper, broccoli florets, mushrooms, and snap peas. Sauté the vegetables for 5-7 minutes, aiming for a tender-crisp texture.
6. Create a savory sauce in a small bowl by whisking together soy sauce, rice vinegar, and cornstarch.
7. Add the cooked tofu and the sauce to the skillet. Toss everything together and cook for 2-3 minutes, until the sauce thickens.
8. Off heat, stir the cooked brown rice noodles into the skillet.
9. Serve the stir-fry garnished with sesame seeds, if desired.

Nutritional breakdown per serving:

Calories: 371 kcal, Protein: 16 grams, Carbohydrates: 49 grams, Fat: 13 grams, Saturated Fat: 2 grams, Cholesterol: 0 milligrams, Sodium: 615 milligrams, Fiber: 5 grams, and Sugar: 0 grams.

BAKED COD WITH MANGO SALSA AND ROASTED ASPARAGUS

- Total Cooking Time: 35 minutes
- Prep Time: 15 minutes
- Servings: 4

Ingredients:

- 4 cod fillets (around 6 oz each)
- 1 tbsp olive oil
- 1/2 tsp dried oregano
- 1/4 tsp garlic powder
- Season to taste with salt and pepper
- 1 ripe mango, peeled and diced
- 1/2 red onion, finely chopped
- 1 jalapeño pepper, seeded and finely chopped for a spicy kick
- 1/4 cup chopped fresh cilantro
- 1 tbsp lime juice
- Season to taste with salt and pepper
- 1 lb asparagus spears, trimmed
- 1 tbsp olive oil
- 1/4 tsp dried thyme
- Season to taste with salt and pepper

Instructions:

1. To commence with the recipe, start by preheating your oven to 400°F (200°C). Line a baking sheet with parchment paper.
2. To enhance flavor, pat cod fillets dry. Create a spice rub by whisking olive oil, oregano, garlic powder, salt, and pepper in a bowl. Gently massage the rub onto both sides of the cod.
3. Wash and trim the asparagus spears. Toss them with olive oil, thyme, salt, and pepper on the prepared baking sheet. Spread the asparagus in a single layer, making sure they are not crowded.
4. Place the baking sheet with asparagus in the preheated oven. Roast for 10-12 minutes, or until tender-crisp and slightly browned.
5. As the asparagus cooks in the oven, whip up a refreshing mango salsa. Combine diced mango, red onion, jalapeno (optional), chopped cilantro, lime

juice, salt, and pepper in a bowl. Toss to coat. Let the flavors meld while the asparagus finishes roasting.

6. After 10-12 minutes of roasting the asparagus, carefully remove the baking sheet from the oven. Arrange the seasoned cod fillets on the same baking sheet, placing them in between the asparagus spears. Pop the baking sheet back in the oven and bake for another 10-12 minutes, or until the cod turns opaque throughout and flakes effortlessly with a fork.

7. Divide the roasted asparagus and cod fillets among plates. Top each serving with a generous portion of the refreshing mango salsa. Enjoy!

Nutritional breakdown per serving:

Calories: 313 kcal, Protein: 34 grams, Carbohydrates: 20 grams, Fat: 12 grams, Saturated Fat: 2 grams, Cholesterol: 75 milligrams, Sodium: 345 milligrams, Fiber: 4 grams, and Sugar: 1 grams.

CHAPTER 4
VEGITARIONS &
SEAFOOD

ROASTED VEGETABLE AND QUINOA BUDDHA BOWL

- Total Cooking Time: 45 minutes
- Prep Time: 15 minutes
- Cook Time: 30 minutes
- Servings: 4

Ingredients:

<u>For the Roasted Vegetables:</u>

- 1 medium sweet potato, peeled and cubed
- 1 inch diced red pepper
- 1 zucchini, halved and sliced into 1/2-inch thick pieces
- 1 cup Brussels sprouts, halved
- 1 red onion, cut into wedges
- 2 tablespoons olive oil
- 1 teaspoon dried thyme
- 1/2 teaspoon salt
- 1/4 teaspoon black pepper
- For the Quinoa:
- 1 cup uncooked quinoa, rinsed
- 2 cups vegetable or chicken broth
- For the Toppings:
- 1 avocado, sliced
- 1/4 cup toasted pumpkin seeds
- 2 tablespoons crumbled feta cheese (optional)
- 2 tablespoons chopped fresh parsley

<u>For the Tahini Dressing:</u>

- 1/4 cup tahini
- 2 tablespoons lemon juice
- 1 tablespoon honey
- 1 garlic clove, minced
- 2-3 tablespoons water, as needed to thin the dressing
- Salt and pepper to taste

Directions:

1. To commence with the recipe, start by preheating your oven to 400°F (200°C). Line two baking sheets with parchment paper.
2. In a large bowl, combine the colorful cubed sweet potato, vibrant bell pepper, tender zucchini, hearty Brussels sprouts, and sliced red onion. Drizzle with olive oil, sprinkle with fragrant dried thyme, and season with salt and pepper. Toss to coat everything well.
3. Spread seasoned veggies on the baking sheet (single layer). Roast in the preheated oven 25-30 minutes for tender-browned veggies (stir halfway).
4. Don't waste time while the vegetables bake! In a saucepan, combine rinsed quinoa with vegetable or chicken broth. Bring the mixture to a boil, then reduce heat, cover, and simmer for 15-20 minutes. Cook until the quinoa reaches a fluffy and tender texture, absorbing all the liquid. Fluff with a fork and set aside.
5. Prepare a flavorful tahini dressing. In a small bowl, whisk together tahini, tangy lemon juice, a touch of honey, and fragrant garlic. Add water to thin it to your liking, and season with salt and pepper for a well-rounded taste.
6. To assemble the Buddha bowls, divide the roasted vegetables and cooked quinoa evenly among 4 serving bowls. Top each bowl with sliced avocado, toasted pumpkin seeds, and crumbled feta cheese (if using). Dress it up! Drizzle the tahini dressing over your creation, and don't forget to garnish with chopped fresh parsley for a final touch.

Nutritional breakdown per serving:

Calories: 425 kcal, Protein: 13 grams, Carbohydrates: 50 grams, Fat: 20 grams, Saturated Fat: 3 grams, Cholesterol: 5 milligrams, Sodium: 540 milligrams, Fiber: 9 grams, and Sugar: 10 grams.

THAI COCONUT CURRY WITH TOFU AND VEGETABLES

- Total Cooking Time: 40 minutes
- Prep Time: 15 minutes
- Cook Time: 25 minutes
- Servings: 4

Ingredients:

- 1 block (14 oz) extra-firm tofu, pressed and cubed
- 2 tablespoons coconut oil
- 1 red bell pepper, sliced
- 1 cup sliced mushrooms
- 1 cup broccoli florets
- 1 cup thinly sliced carrots
- 1 cup thinly sliced zucchini
- 1 medium onion, sliced
- 3 cloves garlic, minced
- 2 tablespoons Thai red curry paste
- 1 cup unsweetened coconut milk
- 1 cup vegetable broth
- 2 teaspoon fish sauce (use soy sauce for vegan)
- 1 tablespoon brown sugar
- 1 teaspoon ground ginger
- 1/4 teaspoon crushed red pepper flakes (optional for added heat)
- 1/4 cup chopped fresh cilantro
- Juice of 1 lime
- Cooked jasmine rice, for serving

Instructions:

1. For crispier tofu, press out excess moisture! Wrap the block in clean kitchen towels or paper towels. Weight the tofu (cast-iron skillet works well) for 15-20 minutes. Then, cut the pressed tofu into 1-inch cubes.
2. Cook the cubed tofu in the pan, stirring occasionally, until it's golden brown and reaches a delicious internal temperature of 160°F (71°C). This ensures safe consumption.Remove cooked tofu from the pan and set aside. (Simple and clear)
3. Add sliced bell pepper, mushrooms, broccoli, carrots, zucchini, and onion to the pan. Sauté 5-7 minutes until softened.

4. Saute the minced garlic in the skillet for 1 minute, allowing it to become fragrant.
5. Stir it into the pan and cook for 1 minute. This short cooking time allows the flavors to "bloom" and intensify.
6. Add the creamy coconut milk and flavorful vegetable broth to the pan. Add the fish sauce (or soy sauce), brown sugar, and ground ginger. Stir to combine.
7. Bring everything to a simmer and let it cook for 10-12 minutes. This simmering step allows the vegetables to soften nicely, while the sauce thickens a bit, resulting in a flavorful and well-balanced dish.
8. Return the cooked tofu to the pan and stir gently to incorporate it with the flavorful sauce. Give the tofu some love! Simmer for another 2-3 minutes, letting it soak up all those delicious flavors from the sauce.
9. Give your creation a final touch! Take the skillet off the heat and stir in the chopped fresh cilantro and a squeeze of tangy lime juice for a burst of color and flavor.
10. Serve the Thai coconut curry over cooked jasmine rice. Enjoy!

Nutritional breakdown per serving:

Calories: 340 kcal, Protein: 15 grams, Carbohydrates: 32 grams, Fat: 20 grams, Saturated Fat: 12 grams, Cholesterol: 0 milligrams, Sodium: 680 milligrams, Fiber: 5 grams, and Sugar: 8 grams.

GRILLED PORTOBELLO MUSHROOM BURGERS WITH AVOCADO AND SPROUTS

- Total Cooking Time: 30 minutes
- Prep Time: 15 minutes
- Cook Time: 15 minutes
- Servings: 4

Ingredients:

- 4 large portobello mushroom caps, stems removed
- 2 tablespoons olive oil
- 1 teaspoon garlic powder
- 1/2 teaspoon dried thyme
- 1/4 teaspoon salt
- 1/4 teaspoon black pepper
- 4 whole-wheat or brioche burger buns, split
- 1 avocado, sliced
- 1 cup alfalfa or broccoli sprouts
- 2 tomatoes, sliced
- 1/4 cup crumbled feta cheese (optional)

For the Garlic Aioli:

- 1/2 cup mayonnaise
- 2 cloves garlic, minced
- 1 tablespoon lemon juice
- 1/4 teaspoon salt
- 1/8 teaspoon black pepper

Instructions:

1. For beautiful searing, preheat your grill or grill pan to medium-high heat.
2. Whisk olive oil, garlic powder, thyme, salt, and pepper in a dish. Toss portobello caps to coat. (Maintains key details)
3. Give the portobellos a smoky kiss! Grill them for 5-7 minutes per side, aiming for tender flesh with light char marks. Once done, transfer them to a plate and set aside.
4. In a small bowl, whisk together mayonnaise, a touch of minced garlic, tangy lemon juice, a pinch of salt, and black pepper. Set this delightful sauce aside.
5. Toast them lightly on the grill for a smoky flavor, or use a toaster for a classic touch.

6. Start by spreading a generous dollop of the garlicky aioli on the bottom bun for a burst of flavor. Top bun with grilled portobello, avocado slices, sprouts, tomato slices, feta cheese (optional).
7. Top the burgers with the upper buns and serve immediately.

Nutritional breakdown per serving:

Calories: 410 kcal, Protein: 10 grams, Carbohydrates: 40 grams, Fat: 25 grams, Saturated Fat: 4 grams, Cholesterol: 15 milligrams, Sodium: 650 milligrams, Fiber: 8 grams, and Sugar: 6 grams.

LENTIL AND SWEET POTATO STUFFED BELL PEPPERS

- Total Cooking Time: 1 hour 10 minutes
- Prep Time: 20 minutes
- Cook Time: 50 minutes
- Servings: 4

Ingredients:

- 4 medium bell peppers (mix of red, yellow, and orange)
- 1 cup dry brown lentils, rinsed
- 2 cups low-sodium vegetable broth
- 1.5 cups diced sweet potato (peeled)
- 1 tablespoon olive oil
- 1 small onion, diced
- 3 cloves garlic, minced
- 1 teaspoon ground cumin
- 1 teaspoon smoked paprika
- 1/2 teaspoon dried oregano
- 1/4 teaspoon crushed red pepper flakes (optional, for heat)
- 1/2 cup shredded cheese (cheddar or vegan)
- 2 tablespoons chopped fresh parsley

Instructions:

1. To commence with the recipe, start by preheating your oven to 375°F (190°C).
2. Cut them in half lengthwise, removing the seeds and membranes for easy filling. Arrange the pepper halves comfortably in a baking dish.
3. Combine them with vegetable broth in a saucepan. Bring to a boil, then reduce heat to maintain a simmer for 15-20 minutes, covered. You'll know they're done when the lentils are tender throughout. Pat them dry and set aside.
4. Combine them with vegetable broth in a saucepan. Bring the mixture to a boil, then reduce heat, cover, and simmer for 15-20 minutes. You'll know they're done when the lentils are tender throughout. Drain any remaining liquid, then set the lentils aside until you're ready to use them in your recipe.
5. Start by adding the diced onion to the skillet and cook for 3-4 minutes, until it becomes translucent. After 3-4 minutes, add garlic and cook 1 minute for fragrance.
6. Infuse the mixture with warm spices! After the onions and garlic become fragrant, stir in the cooked lentils, ground cumin, smoky paprika, and dried oregano. Don't forget

a pinch of crushed red pepper flakes (optional, for a spicy kick). Season with salt and pepper to match your taste preferences. Let the mixture simmer for an extra 2-3 minutes, allowing all the ingredients to marry their flavors for a delicious result.

7. Spoon the lentil and sweet potato mixture into the prepared bell pepper halves, pressing it down gently to compact it.
8. Top each stuffed bell pepper half with a sprinkle of shredded cheddar cheese (or vegan cheese).
9. Bake stuffed peppers (preheated oven) 25-30 minutes for tender peppers and melted cheese.
10. Once baked, carefully remove the stuffed peppers from the oven and garnish them with a sprinkle of chopped fresh parsley. A sprinkle of chopped fresh parsley finishes the dish beautifully, adding a pop of color and a touch of herbal freshness for an inviting look.
11. Serve the lentil and sweet potato stuffed bell peppers warm.

Nutritional breakdown per serving:

Calories: 320 kcal, Protein: 16 grams, Carbohydrates: 46 grams, Fat: 9 grams, Saturated Fat: 3 grams, Cholesterol: 15 milligrams, Sodium: 380 milligrams, Fiber: 12 grams, and Sugar: 9 grams.

BAKED FALAFEL WITH CUCUMBER-TOMATO SALAD AND TAHINI DRESSING

- Total Cooking Time: 40 minutes
- Prep Time: 20 minutes
- Cook Time: 20 minutes
- Servings: 4

Ingredients:

For the Falafel:

- 1 (15-oz) can chickpeas, drained and rinsed
- 1/2 cup fresh parsley, chopped
- 1/4 cup fresh cilantro, chopped
- 2 cloves garlic, minced
- 1 teaspoon ground cumin
- 1/2 teaspoon ground coriander
- 1/2 teaspoon baking soda
- 1/4 teaspoon cayenne pepper (optional)
- 1/4 cup whole wheat breadcrumbs
- 2 tablespoons all-purpose flour
- 1 tablespoon lemon juice
- 1/4 teaspoon salt
- 1/4 teaspoon black pepper

For the Cucumber-Tomato Salad:

- 1 cucumber, diced
- 2 tomatoes, diced
- 1/2 red onion, thinly sliced
- 2 tablespoons chopped fresh parsley
- 1 tablespoon lemon juice
- 1 tablespoon olive oil
- 1/4 teaspoon salt
- 1/4 teaspoon black pepper

For the Tahini Dressing:

- 1/4 cup tahini
- 3 tablespoons water

- 2 tablespoons lemon juice
- 1 clove garlic, minced
- 1/4 teaspoon salt
- 1/8 teaspoon black pepper

Instructions:

1. To commence with the recipe, start by preheating your oven to 400°F (200°C). Line two baking sheets with parchment paper.
2. In a food processor, pulse together the drained and rinsed chickpeas, fresh parsley, cilantro, garlic, cumin, coriander, baking soda, and a touch of cayenne pepper (optional, for a kick). Stop pulsing when the mixture is coarsely chopped, not completely smooth.
3. Transfer the chickpea mixture to a bowl. Now, to bind everything together, stir in the breadcrumbs, flour, lemon juice, salt, and black pepper until well incorporated.
4. Scoop the mixture with heaping tablespoons and roll them into small patties or balls. Arrange them on your prepared baking sheet, leaving space between each one for even cooking and a golden brown finish.
5. Bake falafel (preheated oven) 18-20 minutes, flipping halfway for golden brown crispiness.
6. Combine diced cucumber, tomato, red onion, parsley, lemon juice, olive oil, salt & pepper (medium bowl). Toss, set aside.
7. In a small bowl, whisk together the tahini, water, lemon juice, garlic, salt, and black pepper to make the tahini dressing. Add more water, if needed, to achieve a pourable consistency.
8. To serve, place the baked falafel on a plate or in a pita pocket. Top with the cucumber-tomato salad and drizzle the tahini dressing over the top.

Nutritional breakdown per serving:

Calories: 360 kcal, Protein: 13 grams, Carbohydrates: 40 grams, Fat: 18 grams, Saturated Fat: 2.5 grams, Cholesterol: 0 milligrams, Sodium: 620 milligrams, Fiber: 9 grams, and Sugar: 5 grams.

SEARED AHI TUNA POKE BOWLS WITH EDAMAME AND BROWN RICE

- Total Cooking Time: 30 minutes
- Prep Time: 20 minutes
- Cook Time: 10 minutes
- Servings: 4

Ingredients:

<u>For the Ahi Tuna Poke:</u>

- 1 lb sushi-grade ahi tuna (1/2 inch cubes)
- 2 tablespoons soy sauce
- 1 tablespoon sesame oil
- 1 tablespoon rice vinegar
- 1 teaspoon honey
- 1 teaspoon toasted sesame seeds
- 1/2 teaspoon grated ginger
- 1/4 teaspoon crushed red pepper flakes (optional)

<u>For the Bowls:</u>

- 2 cups cooked brown rice
- 1 cup cooked edamame, chilled
- 1 avocado, diced
- 1 cup shredded carrots
- 2 green onions, thinly sliced
- 2 tablespoons chopped fresh cilantro

<u>For the Poke Dressing:</u>

- 2 tablespoons soy sauce
- 1 tablespoon rice vinegar
- 1 tablespoon sesame oil
- 1 teaspoon honey
- 1/2 teaspoon grated ginger
- Red pepper flakes (optional)

Instructions:

1. In a medium bowl, whisk together 2 tablespoons soy sauce, 1 tablespoon each of sesame oil and rice vinegar, 1 teaspoon honey, and grated ginger. Toss in the cubed ahi tuna (1 lb, cut into ½-inch cubes) and toasted sesame seeds. Add crushed red pepper flakes (optional, for a spicy kick). Gently coat the tuna with the marinade, then cover and refrigerate for 10-15 minutes for extra flavor.

2. In a small bowl, whisk together the dressing ingredients: 2 tablespoons soy sauce, 1 tablespoon each of rice vinegar and sesame oil, 1 teaspoon honey, and 1/2 teaspoon grated ginger. Include crushed red pepper flakes (optional) if you prefer a spicy kick. Set this flavorful sauce aside until you're ready to assemble your poke bowls.

3. Get your pan nice and hot over medium-high heat. Once it's sizzling hot, add the marinated ahi tuna in a single layer. Sear them for 30-60 seconds per side, depending on how cooked you like your tuna. Aim for a crispy sear on the outside while keeping the center rare and cool. Once cooked, transfer it to a cutting board and leave it undisturbed for a few minutes.

4. In a large bowl, place the cooked brown rice as the base. Top with the seared ahi tuna, cooked edamame, diced avocado, shredded carrots, and sliced green onions.

5. Drizzle the poke dressing over the top of the bowls and garnish with chopped fresh cilantro.

6. Serve the Seared Ahi Tuna Poke Bowls immediately, while the tuna is still slightly warm.

Nutritional breakdown per serving:

Calories: 470 kcal, Protein: 30 grams, Carbohydrates: 40 grams, Fat: 20 grams, Saturated Fat: 3 grams, Cholesterol: 40 milligrams, Sodium: 720 milligrams, Fiber: 8 grams, and Sugar: 6 grams.

ROASTED CAULIFLOWER AND CHICKPEA TACOS WITH CREAMY AVOCADO SAUCE

- Total Cooking Time: 40 minutes
- Prep Time: 15 minutes
- Cook Time: 25 minutes
- Servings: 4 (makes 8 tacos)

Ingredients:

For the Roasted Cauliflower and Chickpeas:

- 1 head of cauliflower, cut into small florets (about 4 cups)
- 1 (15-oz) can chickpeas, drained and rinsed
- 2 tablespoons olive oil
- 1 teaspoon ground cumin
- 1 teaspoon chili powder
- 1/2 teaspoon garlic powder
- 1/4 teaspoon salt
- 1/4 teaspoon black pepper
- For the Creamy Avocado Sauce:
- 1 ripe avocado
- 1/4 cup plain Greek yogurt
- 2 tablespoons lime juice
- 1 clove garlic, minced
- 1/4 teaspoon salt
- 1/4 teaspoon black pepper

For the Tacos:

- 8 small corn tortillas
- 1 cup shredded red cabbage
- 1/4 cup chopped fresh cilantro

Instructions:

1. To commence with the recipe, start by preheating your oven to 400°F (200°C). Line two baking sheets with parchment paper.
2. Toss the cauliflower florets and rinsed chickpeas in a large bowl with olive oil, cumin, chili powder, and garlic powder. Season generously with salt and pepper for flavorful roasting.

3. On your prepared baking sheet, spread the seasoned cauliflower and chickpeas in a single layer. This ensures everything gets nice and browned. Roast for 20-25 minutes, giving everything a toss halfway through. Aim for tender cauliflower with lightly browned edges.
4. While the cauliflower and chickpeas are roasting, prepare the creamy avocado sauce. In a food processor or blender, combine the avocado, Greek yogurt, lime juice, garlic, salt, and black pepper. Blend until smooth and creamy. Taste and adjust seasoning as needed.
5. Give those corn tortillas some warmth! Follow the package instructions to heat them up perfectly.
6. In your food processor, blend avocado, Greek yogurt, lime juice, garlic, salt, and pepper until luxuriously smooth. Taste and adjust seasonings for a perfect match with the roasted veggies. This creamy sauce will be the delicious finishing touch!
7. Serve the Roasted Cauliflower and Chickpea Tacos immediately, while the cauliflower and chickpeas are still warm.

Nutritional breakdown per serving:

Calories: 380 kcal, Protein: 12 grams, Carbohydrates: 48 grams, Fat: 16 grams, Saturated Fat: 2.5 grams, Cholesterol: 0 milligrams, Sodium: 560 milligrams, Fiber: 12 grams, and Sugar: 3 grams.

MEDITERRANEAN BAKED COD WITH TOMATOES, OLIVES, AND ARTICHOKES

- Total Cooking Time: 40 minutes
- Prep Time: 15 minutes
- Cook Time: 25 minutes
- Servings: 4

Ingredients:

- 1 lb cod fillets, cut into 4 portions
- 2 tablespoons olive oil
- 1 can diced tomatoes in juice
- 1 can artichoke hearts, drained and halved
- 1/2 cup pitted kalamata olives, halved
- 2 cloves garlic, minced
- 1 teaspoon dried oregano
- 1/2 teaspoon dried basil for added flavor
- 1/4 teaspoon crushed red pepper flakes (optional)
- Salt and black pepper to taste
- 2 tablespoons chopped fresh parsley, for garnish

Instructions:

1. Pop the oven on to preheat at 400°F (200°C) while you prep the remaining ingredients. Grease a 9x13 inch baking dish or oven-safe skillet with 1 tablespoon of the olive oil.
2. Nestle the cod fillets in your prepared baking dish or skillet. Then, give them a flavor boost with a generous sprinkle of salt and black pepper.
3. In a medium bowl, bring together the remaining olive oil, diced tomatoes (including their juices), artichoke hearts, kalamata olives, minced garlic, and the dried herbs (oregano and basil). Give everything in the bowl a good toss to combine. If you like a touch of heat, sprinkle in some crushed red pepper flakes while you toss.
4. Spoon the tomato-artichoke-olive mixture over and around the cod fillets, making sure the fish is mostly covered.
5. Pop the cod in the preheated oven and bake for 20-25 minutes. Bake for 20-25 minutes, or until the cod is opaque and flakes easily with a fork. This ensures perfectly cooked, moist fish!
6. Take your beautiful baked cod out of the oven. Sprinkle it with chopped fresh parsley for a pop of color and freshness – the perfect finishing touch!

7. Serve the Mediterranean Baked Cod immediately, spooning the tomato-artichoke-olive sauce over the top of the fish.

Nutritional breakdown per serving:

Calories: 280 kcal, Protein: 28 grams, Carbohydrates: 15 grams, Fat: 13 grams, Saturated Fat: 2 grams, Cholesterol: 60 milligrams, Sodium: 760 milligrams, Fiber: 5 grams, and Sugar: 3 grams.

QUINOA AND VEGETABLE STIR-FRY WITH GINGER-GARLIC SAUCE

- Total Cooking Time: 30 minutes
- Prep Time: 15 minutes
- Cook Time: 15 minutes
- Servings: 4

Ingredients:

For the Stir-Fry:

- 1 cup uncooked quinoa, rinsed
- 2 cups low-sodium vegetable broth
- 2 tablespoons sesame oil
- 2 cups chopped vegetables (broccoli, carrots, peppers, peas)
- 1 cup sliced mushrooms
- 1 cup cooked edamame
- 2 green onions, thinly sliced
- 2 tablespoons toasted sesame seeds (for garnish)

For the Ginger-Garlic Sauce:

- 2 tablespoons low-sodium soy sauce
- 2 tablespoons rice vinegar
- 1 tablespoon honey
- 1 tablespoon freshly grated ginger
- 2 cloves garlic, minced
- 1 teaspoon cornstarch
- 1/4 teaspoon red pepper flakes (optional)

Instructions:

1. In a saucepan, simmer rinsed quinoa with vegetable broth for 15-20 minutes, or until fluffy and cooked through. Fluff with a fork and set aside. This will be the base for your tasty dish!
2. Wash and chop the broccoli, carrots, bell peppers, and snow peas. Slice the mushrooms. Slice the green onions.
3. In a bowl, whisk soy sauce, rice vinegar, honey, ginger, garlic, and cornstarch. Add red pepper flakes for a kick (optional). Set aside - this tasty sauce will be used later!
4. Get your wok or skillet scorching hot over medium-high heat. Drizzle in sesame oil to coat the bottom.

5. Add the prepared vegetables and stir-fry for 5-7 minutes, or until the vegetables are tender-crisp.
6. Add the cooked quinoa and edamame to the stir-fried vegetables. Pour the Ginger-Garlic Sauce over the mixture and toss to coat everything evenly.
7. Cook for 2-3 more minutes, or until the sauce reaches your desired consistency.
8. Serve the Quinoa and Vegetable Stir-Fry immediately, garnished with the toasted sesame seeds.

Nutritional breakdown per serving:

Calories: 320 kcal, Protein: 14 grams, Carbohydrates: 44 grams, Fat: 11 grams, Saturated Fat: 1.5 grams, Cholesterol: 0 milligrams, Sodium: 460 milligrams, Fiber: 7 grams, and Sugar: 7 grams.

BAKED TOFU AND BROCCOLI STIR-FRY WITH BROWN RICE NOODLES

- Total Cooking Time: 45 minutes
- Prep Time: 20 minutes
- Cook Time: 25 minutes
- Servings: 4

Ingredients:

<u>For the Tofu:</u>

- 1 block (14 oz) extra-firm tofu, pressed and cubed
- 2 tablespoons low-sodium soy sauce
- 1 tablespoon rice vinegar
- 1 tablespoon sesame oil
- 1 teaspoon cornstarch
- For the Stir-Fry:
- 8 oz brown rice noodles
- 2 tablespoons vegetable oil, divided
- 3 cups broccoli florets
- 1 red bell pepper, sliced
- 2 cloves garlic, minced
- 1 tablespoon freshly grated ginger
- 2 tablespoons low-sodium soy sauce
- 1 tablespoon rice vinegar
- 1 tablespoon honey
- 1 teaspoon sesame oil
- 1/4 teaspoon red pepper flakes (optional)
- 2 green onions, thinly sliced (for garnish)
- 2 tablespoons toasted sesame seeds (for garnish)

Instructions:

1. Pop the oven on to preheat at 400°F (200°C) while you prep the remaining ingredients.
2. In a bowl, toss cubed tofu with soy sauce, rice vinegar, sesame oil, and cornstarch. Once coated, spread the tofu on a baking sheet and pop it in the oven. Bake for 20-25 minutes, flipping halfway through. Aim for nice golden brown edges and a crispy texture!

3. Cook the brown rice noodles following the package directions. Once done, drain them well and set them aside for later.
4. Heat a drizzle of oil in your large skillet or wok over medium-high. Once hot, add the broccoli florets and stir-fry for 3-4 minutes until they reach tender-crisp perfection with a bright green hue. Set them aside on a plate for now.
5. Once the pan is clear (after removing the broccoli), add the remaining tablespoon of oil. Toss in the sliced red bell pepper, minced garlic, and grated ginger. Stir-fry for 2-3 minutes, letting the delicious aromas fill your kitchen!
6. Once the aromatics are fragrant, add the cooked brown rice noodles, baked tofu, and cooked broccoli back to the pan. Pour in the stir-fry sauce (2 tbsp soy sauce, 1 tbsp rice vinegar, 1 tbsp honey, 1 tsp sesame oil) and toss everything together until well coated.
7. If using, sprinkle the red pepper flakes over the stir-fry.
8. Cook for an additional 2-3 minutes, or until the noodles are heated through and the sauce has thickened slightly.
9. For a finishing touch, garnish your stir-fry with sliced green onions and toasted sesame seeds. They'll add a burst of fresh flavor and a delightful crunch!
10. Serve immediately while hot.

Nutritional breakdown per serving:

Calories: 380 kcal, Protein: 18 grams, Carbohydrates: 47 grams, Fat: 15 grams, Saturated Fat: 2grams, Cholesterol: 0 milligrams, Sodium: 680 milligrams, Fiber: 7 grams, and Sugar: 7 grams.

GRILLED SALMON AND ASPARAGUS FOIL PACKETS WITH LEMON-DILL SAUCE

- Total Cooking Time: 30 minutes
  Prep Time: 15 minutes
  Cook Time: 15 minutes
  Servings: 4

Ingredients:

For the Foil Packets:

- 4 (6 oz) salmon fillets, skin removed
- 1 lb asparagus spears, trimmed
- 2 tablespoons olive oil
- 1 teaspoon lemon zest
- Salt and pepper to taste

For the Lemon-Dill Sauce:

- 1/4 cup plain Greek yogurt
- 2 tablespoons freshly squeezed lemon juice
- 2 tablespoons chopped fresh dill
- 1 clove garlic, minced
- 1/4 teaspoon salt
- 1/8 teaspoon black pepper

Instructions:

1. Heat up your grill for searing success! Aim for medium-high heat.
2. Prepare four squares of heavy-duty aluminum foil, each measuring 12 inches by 12 inches. Place one salmon fillet and a quarter of the asparagus spears on each foil square. Dress your salmon and asparagus with a touch of olive oil, then sprinkle on some lemon zest, salt, and pepper for a burst of flavor.
3. Take a sheet of aluminum foil and place it over the salmon and asparagus. Crimp the edges of the foil together to create a sealed packet.
4. Once the foil packets have been sealed, position them on the grill that has been preheated. Allow the contents to cook for 12 to 15 minutes, or until the salmon has fully cooked and the asparagus has become tender.
5. While the foil packets are cooking, prepare the Lemon-Dill Sauce. In a small bowl, whisk together the Greek yogurt, lemon juice, chopped dill, minced garlic, salt, and black pepper. Cover and refrigerate until ready to serve.

6. Cautiously take the foil-wrapped packets off the grill and transfer them onto serving dishes.
7. Serve the Grilled Salmon and Asparagus Foil Packets with the Lemon-Dill Sauce on the side.

Nutritional breakdown per serving:

Calories: 290 kcal, Protein: 30 grams, Carbohydrates: 8 grams, Fat: 15 grams, Saturated Fat: 3 grams, Cholesterol: 70 milligrams, Sodium: 450 milligrams, Fiber: 3 grams, and Sugar: 3 grams.

ROASTED BUTTERNUT SQUASH AND KALE LASAGNA

- Total Cooking Time: 1 hour 20 minutes
- Prep Time: 30 minutes
- Cook Time: 50 minutes
- Servings: 8

Ingredients:

For the Butternut Squash Filling:

- 4 cups cubed butternut squash (peeled & seeded)
- 2 tablespoons olive oil
- 1 teaspoon dried sage
- 1/2 teaspoon salt
- 1/4 teaspoon black pepper
- For the Kale Filling:
- 4 cups chopped kale (discard stems)
- 1 tablespoon olive oil
- 2 cloves garlic, minced
- 1/4 teaspoon red pepper flakes (optional)
- 1/4 teaspoon salt

For the Lasagna:

- 9 no-boil lasagna noodles
- 1 1/2 cups part-skim ricotta cheese
- 1 1/2 cups shredded part-skim mozzarella, divided
- 1/2 cup grated Parmesan cheese
- 1 egg
- 1/4 teaspoon salt
- 1/4 teaspoon black pepper

Instructions:

1. Pop the oven on to preheat at 400°F (200°C) while you prep the remaining ingredients.
2. Arrange the cubed butternut squash in a large baking dish. Coat the squash with olive oil. Then, add a sprinkle of dried sage, salt, and black pepper. This phrasing uses different verbs and avoids mentioning specific amounts. Roast the seasoned squash in

the oven for 25 to 30 minutes, until it becomes tender and develops a light browning. Take the baking dish out of the oven and let it sit to allow the contents to cool.

3. Set a large skillet over medium heat and pour in 1 tablespoon of olive oil. After the oil in the large skillet has heated up, toss in the chopped kale, minced garlic, and red pepper flakes (if using). Sauté for 5-7 minutes, or until the kale is wilted and tender. Season with 1/4 teaspoon of salt. Remove from heat and set aside.

4. Take a medium-sized bowl and mix together the ricotta cheese, 1 cup of mozzarella cheese, Parmesan cheese, egg, 1/4 teaspoon of salt, and 1/4 teaspoon of black pepper. Mix all the ingredients together thoroughly, then set the bowl aside.

5. Dial down the oven temperature to 375°F (190°C).

6. Evenly spread 1/2 cup of the ricotta cheese mixture across the bottom of a 9x13-inch baking dish.

7. Layer 3 more lasagna noodles over the previous ingredients.

8. Evenly distribute the remaining ricotta cheese mixture on top of the noodles.

9. For the next layer, arrange 3 lasagna noodles.

10. Dollop or spread the leftover ricotta cheese mixture on the noodles.

11. Top with the remaining butternut squash and kale.

12. Cover with the final 3 lasagna noodles.

13. Sprinkle the remaining 1/2 cup of mozzarella cheese over the top.

14. Following the recipe's temperature instructions, bake the dish covered with foil for 30 minutes.

15. Carefully wrap the baking dish in aluminum foil and put it into the preheated oven. Let it bake for 30 minutes. Next, take off the aluminum foil covering and let the dish bake for another 20 minutes, or until the cheese has fully melted and is bubbling.

16. After baking, permit the lasagna to sit for 10-15 minutes before slicing and serving.

Nutritional breakdown per serving:

Calories: 345 kcal, Protein: 19 grams, Carbohydrates: 41 grams, Fat: 13 grams, Saturated Fat: 6 grams, Cholesterol: 55 milligrams, Sodium: 580 milligrams, Fiber: 6 grams, and Sugar: 5 grams.

MISO GLAZED SALMON WITH ROASTED BRUSSELS SPROUTS

- Total Cooking Time: 40 minutes
- Prep Time: 15 minutes
- Cook Time: 25 minutes
- Servings: 4

Ingredients:

For the Miso Glazed Salmon:

- 4 (6 oz) salmon fillets
- 3 tablespoons white miso paste
- 2 tablespoons honey
- 2 tablespoons rice vinegar
- 1 tablespoon soy sauce
- 1 teaspoon sesame oil
- 1 teaspoon grated fresh ginger
- For the Roasted Brussels Sprouts:
- 1 lb Brussels sprouts, trimmed and halved
- 2 tablespoons olive oil
- 1/2 teaspoon salt
- 1/4 teaspoon black pepper

Instructions:

1. Pop the oven on to preheat at 400°F (200°C) while you prep the remaining ingredients.
2. In a small bowl, whisk together the white miso paste, honey, rice vinegar, soy sauce, sesame oil, and grated ginger until well combined. Position the salmon fillets in a baking dish, then use a brush to apply the miso glaze evenly over the top of each fillet. Leave the prepared dish to the side.
3. In a large baking sheet, toss the trimmed and halved Brussels sprouts with the olive oil, salt, and black pepper until well coated. Distribute the Brussels sprouts across the baking sheet in a single even layer.
4. Place the baking dish with the miso-glazed salmon and the baking sheet with the Brussels sprouts in the preheated oven. Roast the dish for 18-22 minutes, or until the salmon is fully cooked and the Brussels sprouts are tender with a light browning.
5. Remove the salmon and Brussels sprouts from the oven.

6. Serve the Miso Glazed Salmon fillets immediately, with the roasted Brussels sprouts on the side.

Nutritional breakdown per serving:

Calories: 380 kcal, Protein: 35 grams, Carbohydrates: 20 grams, Fat: 17 grams, Saturated Fat: 3 grams, Cholesterol: 80 milligrams, Sodium: 790 milligrams, Fiber: 5 grams, and Sugar: 11 grams.

VEGETABLE AND TOFU LETTUCE WRAPS WITH PEANUT SAUCE

- Total Cooking Time: 30 minutes
- Prep Time: 15 minutes
- Servings: 4

Ingredients:

- 1 block (14 oz) extra-firm tofu, pressed and drained
- 1 tbsp soy sauce
- 1 tbsp cornstarch
- 1/2 tsp sriracha (or chili flakes for a milder option)
- 1/2 tsp sesame oil
- 1/4 tsp garlic powder
- 1/4 tsp ground ginger
- 1 red bell pepper, thinly sliced
- 1 yellow bell pepper, thinly sliced
- 1 cup shredded carrots
- 1/2 cup chopped red onion
- 1/4 cup chopped fresh cilantro
- 1 head of romaine lettuce, washed and separated
- 1/3 cup creamy peanut butter
- 1/4 cup low-sodium soy sauce
- 1 tbsp rice vinegar
- 1 tbsp honey (or agave nectar for a vegan option)
- 1 tbsp Sriracha (or chili flakes for a milder option)
- 1 tbsp lime juice
- 1 clove garlic, minced
- 1/4 cup water (add more for a thinner consistency)

Instructions:

1. For fluffier quinoa, let it steam off excess moisture for 15+ minutes. Wrap the pot in a clean kitchen towel.
2. Let the tofu press while you mix up the marinade. In a shallow dish, combine soy sauce, cornstarch, sriracha (or chili flakes) for a kick, sesame oil, garlic powder, and ground ginger. After pressing, cube the tofu and let it soak up the delicious marinade. Toss to coat evenly and let marinate for at least 10 minutes, or up to 30 minutes for deeper flavor.

3. Wash and thinly slice the bell peppers. Shred the carrots and chop the red onion and fresh cilantro. Set aside in separate bowls.
4. Get a big pan on the stovetop and heat it up to medium. Once it's nice and hot, add a drizzle of oil to coat the surface. Once hot, add the marinated tofu cubes and cook, turning occasionally, for 5-7 minutes per side. They're ready when golden brown and crispy!
5. In a small bowl, whisk together creamy peanut butter, soy sauce, rice vinegar, honey (or agave nectar), sriracha (or chili flakes), lime juice, and minced garlic. Gradually whisk in water, a little at a time, until the sauce reaches your perfect consistency.
6. Turn those romaine leaves into delicious boats! Arrange them on a platter and fill each one with a dollop of cooked tofu, a vibrant mix of colorful veggies, and a drizzle of creamy peanut sauce. Dig in!

Nutritional breakdown per serving:

Calories: 295 kcal, Protein: 18 grams, Carbohydrates: 19 grams, Fat: 18 grams, Saturated Fat: 3 grams, Cholesterol: 0 milligrams, Sodium: 720 milligrams, Fiber: 5 grams, and Sugar: 8 grams.

BAKED COD TACOS WITH CABBAGE SLAW AND AVOCADO

- Total Cooking Time: 35 minute
- Prep Time: 20 minutes
- Cook Time: 15 minutes
- Servings: 4 (3 tacos per serving)

Ingredients:

- 1 lb cod fillets, cut into 1-inch cubes
- 2 tablespoons olive oil
- 1 teaspoon chili powder
- 1/2 teaspoon ground cumin
- 1/2 teaspoon garlic powder
- 1/4 teaspoon salt
- 1/4 teaspoon black pepper
- 2 cups shredded green cabbage
- 1 cup shredded red cabbage
- 1/2 cup thinly sliced red onion
- 2 tablespoons chopped fresh cilantro
- 2 tablespoons lime juice
- 1 tablespoon olive oil
- 1/4 teaspoon salt
- 1/4 teaspoon black pepper
- 12 small corn tortillas, warmed
- 1 avocado, sliced

Instructions:

1. Pop the oven on to preheat at 400°F (200°C) while you prep the remaining ingredients.
2. In a large bowl, toss the cubed cod with the olive oil, chili powder, cumin, garlic powder, salt, and black pepper until the fish is evenly coated.
3. Spread the seasoned cod cubes in a single layer on a parchment-lined baking sheet.
4. Bake for 12-15 minutes, letting the cod cook until it's flaky and reaches a beautiful white color. A fork should be able to break it apart with no resistance.
5. In a medium bowl, combine the shredded green cabbage, shredded red cabbage, thinly sliced red onion, and chopped fresh cilantro.

6. Make a simple dressing in a small bowl. Whisk together the lime juice, olive oil, a pinch of salt, and some black pepper.
7. Give the cabbage mixture a good toss with the dressing to make sure everything gets coated.
8. Give the corn tortillas some warmth! Follow the heating method on the package.
9. Place a few pieces of the baked cod in the center of each tortilla.
10. Top the cod with a generous amount of the cabbage slaw.
11. Garnish each taco with sliced avocado.
12. Serve the Baked Cod Tacos immediately, allowing your guests to customize their tacos with the desired fillings.

Nutritional breakdown per serving:

Calories: 390 kcal, Protein: 27 grams, Carbohydrates: 38 grams, Fat: 16 grams, Saturated Fat: 2.5 grams, Cholesterol: 55 milligrams, Sodium: 520 milligrams, Fiber: 8 grams, and Sugar: 3 grams.

ROASTED VEGETABLE AND HUMMUS FLATBREAD

- Total Cooking Time: 35 minutes
- Prep Time: 15 minutes
- Servings: 4

Ingredients:

- 1 red bell pepper, sliced
- 1 yellow bell pepper, sliced
- 1 zucchini, sliced
- 1 red onion, sliced
- 1 tablespoon olive oil
- 1/2 teaspoon dried thyme
- Season with salt and pepper
- 4 whole wheat pita breads
- 2 tablespoons olive oil
- 1 cup hummus (any flavor)
- 1/4 cup crumbled feta cheese (optional)
- 1/4 cup chopped fresh parsley

Instructions:

1. Preheat it to 400°F (200°C) while you prep the rest of your ingredients. To save on cleanup, line a baking sheet with parchment paper.
2. Wash and slice the bell peppers, zucchini, and red onion. In a large bowl, toss the vegetables with olive oil, thyme, salt, and pepper. Evenly distribute the seasoned veggies across the prepared baking sheet in a single layer.
3. Place the baking sheet with vegetables in the preheated oven. Roast for 20-25 minutes, or until the vegetables are tender-crisp and slightly browned.
4. While the vegetables roast, heat a large skillet or griddle over medium heat. Brush each pita bread with a thin layer of olive oil. Place the pita breads one at a time on the hot skillet and cook for 1-2 minutes per side, or until lightly toasted and warmed through.
5. Dollop a generous amount of hummus onto each warmed pita bread. Top with roasted vegetables, crumbled feta cheese (if using), and chopped fresh parsley.
6. Cut each flatbread into wedges or triangles for easy sharing. Enjoy!

Nutritional breakdown per serving:

Calories: 410 kcal, Protein: 14 grams, Carbohydrates: 46 grams, Fat: 19 grams, Saturated Fat: 5 grams, Cholesterol: 20 milligrams, Sodium: 670 milligrams, Fiber: 8 grams, and Sugar: 5 grams.

GRILLED SHRIMP AND MANGO SALAD WITH LIME-CILANTRO DRESSING

- Total Cooking Time: 30 minutes
- Prep Time: 20 minutes
- Cook Time: 10 minutes
- Servings: 4

Ingredients:

For the Salad:

- 1 lb large shrimp, peeled and deveined
- 1 ripe mango, diced
- 1 cup halved cherry tomatoes
- 1 avocado, diced
- 4 cups mixed greens (such as spinach, arugula, and baby kale)
- 1/4 cup thinly sliced red onion
- For the Lime-Cilantro Dressing:
- 2 tablespoons olive oil
- 2 tablespoons lime juice (about 1 lime)
- 1 tablespoon honey
- 2 tablespoons chopped fresh cilantro
- 1 garlic clove, minced
- 1/4 teaspoon salt
- 1/4 teaspoon black pepper

Instructions:

1. Fire up your grill or grill pan and get it nice and hot over medium-high heat.
2. Thread the shrimp onto skewers, allowing some space in between.
3. Give the shrimp a brush of olive oil and season them with salt and pepper.
4. Grill the shrimp for 2-3 minutes per side, flipping once. They're done when they turn opaque and pink. Let them rest off the heat.
5. For the dressing, whisk olive oil, lime juice, honey, chopped cilantro, minced garlic, salt, and pepper together in a small bowl.
6. Build your salad in a large bowl with mixed greens, diced mango, halved cherry tomatoes, diced avocado, and thinly sliced red onion.
7. Dress the salad with the Lime-Cilantro Dressing, tossing gently to coat everything. Then, arrange the grilled shrimp on top.
8. Divide the Grilled Shrimp and Mango Salad evenly among 4 plates or bowls.

9. This lets everyone savor the freshness and delightful textures in the salad.

Nutritional breakdown per serving:

Calories: 320 kcal, Protein: 22 grams, Carbohydrates: 26 grams, Fat: 15 grams, Saturated Fat: 2.5 grams, Cholesterol: 170 milligrams, Sodium: 550 milligrams, Fiber: 6 grams, and Sugar: 16 grams.

CURRIED LENTIL AND SWEET POTATO SOUP

- Total Cooking Time: 1 hour
- Prep Time: 15 minutes
- Cook Time: 45 minutes
- Servings: 6

Ingredients:

- 1 tablespoon olive oil
- 1 large onion, diced
- 3 garlic cloves, minced
- 2 tablespoons grated fresh ginger
- 2 teaspoons mild curry powder
- 1 teaspoon ground cumin
- 1/4 teaspoon cayenne pepper
- 1/4 teaspoon cayenne pepper, 1 lb sweet potatoes, diced into 1-inch cubes
- 1 cup dried red lentils, rinsed
- 4 cups vegetable broth
- 1 (14 oz) can diced tomatoes
- 1 cup unsweetened coconut milk
- 1 tablespoon fresh lime juice
- Salt and black pepper to taste
- Chopped cilantro for garnish (optional)

Instructions:

1. Set your stovetop to medium heat. In a large pot or Dutch oven, watch the olive oil shimmer as it warms up. Cook the diced onions, stirring occasionally, until they have softened and become translucent, about 5-7 minutes.
2. Toss the minced garlic and grated ginger into the pot. Let the enticing aroma develop for 1 minute, stirring frequently.
3. Add the curry powder, cumin, and cayenne pepper, stirring them into the pot. Let them sizzle and release their fragrance for 1 minute.
4. Start by adding the diced sweet potatoes, rinsed lentils, and vegetable broth to your pot. Then, pour in the diced tomatoes along with their juices.
5. Start by bringing your mixture to a boil. Then, lower the heat to low. Cover the pot and simmer until the ingredients are tender. Alternatively, simmer until the lentils and sweet potatoes are tender when pierced with a fork.

6. Give your soup a luscious touch by stirring in the coconut milk and lime juice. Now that it's simmered, taste your creation and adjust the seasonings to make the flavors burst!
7. Ladle the Curried Lentil and Sweet Potato Soup into bowls. Garnish with chopped cilantro, if desired.
8. Serve the soup hot, accompanied by crusty bread or naan for dipping.

Nutritional breakdown per serving:

Calories: 310 kcal, Protein: 12 grams, Carbohydrates: 44 grams, Fat: 9 grams, Saturated Fat: 5 grams, Cholesterol: 0 milligrams, Sodium: 590 milligrams, Fiber: 9 grams, and Sugar: 8 grams.

SEARED TUNA NIÇOISE SALAD WITH ROASTED POTATOES

- Total Cooking Time: 40 minutes
- Prep Time: 15 minutes
- Servings: 4

Ingredients:

- 2 tuna steaks (each about 6 oz)
- 1 tablespoon olive oil
- 1/2 teaspoon black pepper
- 1/4 teaspoon sea salt
- 1 pound small baby potatoes, halved or quartered if larger
- 1 tablespoon olive oil
- 1/2 teaspoon dried rosemary
- 1/4 teaspoon garlic powder
- Season with salt and pepper
- 1 cup green beans, trimmed and halved
- 1 cup cherry tomatoes, halved
- 1/2 cup pitted Kalamata olives, halved
- 2 hard-boiled eggs, quartered
- 1/4 cup chopped fresh parsley
- 2 tablespoons olive oil
- 1 tablespoon lemon juice
- 1 teaspoon Dijon mustard
- 1/2 teaspoon honey
- 1/4 teaspoon dried oregano
- Season with salt and pepper

Instructions:

1. Preheat it to 400°F (200°C) while you prep the rest of your ingredients. Line a baking sheet with parchment paper.
2. On a baking sheet, toss the halved or quartered potatoes with olive oil, rosemary, garlic powder, salt, and pepper. Scatter the seasoned potatoes on a single layer.
3. Place the baking sheet with potatoes in the preheated oven. Bake for 20-25 minutes, or until golden brown and fork-tender. Give the potatoes a flip halfway through to achieve consistent browning.

4. While the potatoes roast, whisk together olive oil, lemon juice, Dijon mustard, honey, oregano, salt, and pepper in a small bowl. Set aside.
5. Steam or blanch the green beans for 3-5 minutes, or until tender-crisp. For a crisp finish, drain the pasta and rinse it under cool running water.
6. Dry the tuna steaks with paper towels. Press black pepper and sea salt generously onto both surfaces of the tuna.
7. Heat a large skillet over medium-high heat. Add a drizzle of olive oil. Once hot, carefully place the tuna steaks in the pan. Sear for 2-3 minutes per side, or until desired doneness is reached (rare, medium-rare, or well-done).
8. Assemble a delicious medley in a large bowl: roasted potatoes, cooked green beans, halved cherry tomatoes, Kalamata olives, quartered hard-boiled eggs, and a sprinkle of fresh parsley.
9. For a burst of flavor, drizzle the lemon vinaigrette over the salad and toss with a light touch.
10. Divide the salad among plates. Top each serving with a seared tuna steak. Enjoy!

Nutritional breakdown per serving:

Calories: 450 kcal, Protein: 29 grams, Carbohydrates: 31 grams, Fat: 25 grams, Saturated Fat: 4 grams, Cholesterol: 155 milligrams, Sodium: 680 milligrams, Fiber: 5 grams, and Sugar: 6 grams.

BAKED TOFU AND BROCCOLI STIR-FRY WITH BROWN RICE

- Total Cooking Time: 45 minutes
- Prep Time: 15 minutes
- Cook Time: 30 minutes
- Servings: 4

Ingredients:

For the Baked Tofu:

- 1 block (14 oz) extra-firm tofu, pressed and cubed
- 2 tablespoons low-sodium soy sauce
- 1 tablespoon rice vinegar
- 1 tablespoon maple syrup
- 1 teaspoon sesame oil
- 1/4 teaspoon red pepper flakes (optional)

For the Stir-Fry:

- 2 cups broccoli florets
- 1 red bell pepper, thinly sliced
- 3 garlic cloves, minced
- 1 tablespoon grated fresh ginger
- 2 tablespoons low-sodium soy sauce
- 1 tablespoon rice vinegar
- 1 teaspoon sesame oil
- 1/4 cup low-sodium vegetable broth

For the Brown Rice:

- 1 cup uncooked brown rice
- 2 cups low-sodium vegetable broth

Instructions:

1. Assemble your ingredients while preheating the oven to 400°F (200°C).
2. To marinate the tofu, whisk together 2 tablespoons soy sauce, 1 tablespoon rice vinegar, 1 tablespoon maple syrup, and 1 teaspoon sesame oil in a medium bowl. Gently fold in the cubed tofu, ensuring all sides are coated in the flavorful marinade. Sprinkle in some red pepper flakes and toss again.
3. Arrange the marinated tofu cubes in a single layer on a parchment-lined baking sheet.

4. Bake for 20-25 minutes, flipping the tofu halfway through, until crispy and lightly browned. Set aside.
5. In a medium saucepan, combine the uncooked brown rice and 2 cups of low-sodium vegetable broth.
6. Heat your mixture to a boil. Simmer tightly for 20-25 minutes (or until tender). The rice is done when fluffy and the liquid is absorbed.
7. Get your large skillet or wok nice and hot by heating 1 tablespoon of vegetable broth over medium-high heat.
8. Toss in the broccoli florets and sliced red bell pepper. Stir-fry for 4-5 minutes, aiming for crisp-tender veggies.
9. Introduce the aromatic flavors by adding the minced garlic and grated ginger. Stir-fry for another minute until you can smell their fragrance.
10. Whisk together a flavorful sauce in a small bowl: 2 tablespoons soy sauce, 1 tablespoon rice vinegar, and 1 teaspoon sesame oil. Drizzle the sauce over the vegetables in the skillet and give everything a good toss to make sure they're all nicely coated.
11. Add the baked tofu cubes and the remaining 1/4 cup of vegetable broth. Stir to combine and heat through, about 2-3 minutes.
12. Divide the cooked brown rice among 4 plates or bowls.
13. Top the rice with the baked tofu and broccoli stir-fry.
14. Dig in while it's hot! This stir-fry is both delicious and packed with nutrients.

Nutritional breakdown per serving:

Calories: 360 kcal, Protein: 18 grams, Carbohydrates: 51 grams, Fat: 10 grams, Saturated Fat: 1.5 grams, Cholesterol: 0 milligrams, Sodium: 680 milligrams, Fiber: 7 grams, and Sugar: 6 grams.

GRILLED SALMON AND ASPARAGUS SALAD WITH LEMON VINAIGRETTE

- Total Cooking Time: 30 minutes
- Prep Time: 15 minutes
- Cook Time: 15 minutes
- Servings: 4

Ingredients:

For the Salmon and Asparagus:

- 4 (4-oz) salmon fillets
- 1 pound fresh asparagus, trimmed
- 1 tablespoon olive oil
- 1/2 teaspoon salt
- 1/4 teaspoon black pepper

For the Lemon Vinaigrette:

- 3 tablespoons olive oil
- 2 tablespoons lemon juice
- 1 tablespoon Dijon mustard
- 1 garlic clove, minced
- 1 teaspoon honey
- 1/4 teaspoon salt
- 1/8 teaspoon black pepper

For the Salad:

- 5 cups mixed greens (spinach, arugula, lettuce)
- 1 cup cherry tomatoes, halved
- 1/4 cup sliced cucumber
- 2 tablespoons crumbled feta cheese

Instructions:

1. Fire up your grill or grill pan to a sizzling medium-high heat.
2. Lightly coat the salmon fillets and asparagus spears with 1 tablespoon of olive oil. Sprinkle them generously with salt and freshly cracked black pepper.
3. Grill the salmon for 4-6 minutes per side, or until it flakes easily with a fork. Throw the asparagus on the grill and cook for 5-7 minutes, turning them every now and then, until they're nice and tender-crisp.

214

4. Take the cooked salmon and asparagus off the grill and set them aside on a plate.
5. In a small bowl, grab your whisk and combine 3 tablespoons of olive oil, lemon juice, Dijon mustard, minced garlic, honey, salt, and black pepper. Make sure it's all well mixed!
6. Create a beautiful salad by arranging the mixed greens in a large bowl, then scattering the cherry tomatoes and sliced cucumber over them.
7. Finish the salad by drizzling the lemon vinaigrette over it and gently tossing everything together until the greens are lightly coated.
8. Flake the juicy grilled salmon into bite-sized pieces and gently fold them into the salad.
9. Gently fold the salad again to weave the salmon pieces throughout.
10. Top the salad with the grilled asparagus spears and the crumbled feta cheese.
11. Divide the Grilled Salmon and Asparagus Salad among 4 plates or bowls.
12. Serve immediately and enjoy this refreshing and nutrient-rich meal.

Nutritional breakdown per serving:

Calories: 365 kcal, Protein: 32 grams, Carbohydrates: 11 grams, Fat: 22 grams, Saturated Fat: 4 grams, Cholesterol: 65 milligrams, Sodium: 610 milligrams, Fiber: 4 grams, and Sugar: 4 grams.

ROASTED VEGETABLE AND GOAT CHEESE FRITTATA

- Total Cooking Time: 45 minutes
- Prep Time: 20 minutes
- Cook Time: 25 minutes
- Servings: 6

Ingredients:

For the Roasted Vegetables:

- 1 medium zucchini, diced
- 1 red bell pepper, diced
- 1 cup diced mushrooms
- 1 medium red onion, diced
- 2 tablespoons olive oil
- 1/2 teaspoon salt
- 1/4 teaspoon black pepper

For the Frittata:

- 8 large eggs
- 1/4 cup milk
- 1/2 teaspoon dried thyme
- 1/4 teaspoon salt
- 1/8 teaspoon black pepper
- 4 ounces crumbled goat cheese
- 2 tablespoons freshly chopped parsley

Instructions:

1. To commence with the recipe, start by preheating your oven to 400°F (200°C).
2. On a large baking sheet, toss together the diced zucchini, bell pepper, mushrooms, and red onion. After tossing the vegetables, drizzle them with 2 tablespoons of olive oil. Then, sprinkle on 1/2 teaspoon of salt and 1/4 teaspoon of black pepper.
3. Roast the vegetables for 18-20 minutes, stirring halfway, until they are tender and lightly browned. Remove from the oven and set aside.
4. Pop your oven on and preheat it to 375°F (190°C).
5. Crack the eggs into a large bowl. Add the milk, dried thyme, salt (1/4 teaspoon), and pepper (1/8 teaspoon) and whisk everything together until well combined.

6. Grease a 9-inch oven-safe skillet (or a 9-inch pie dish) with a small amount of olive oil or non-stick cooking spray.
7. Spread the roasted vegetables evenly in the prepared skillet or pie dish.
8. Tilt the pan as you slowly pour in the egg mixture, letting it flow around the vegetables and ensuring they're all nestled in a delicious eggy blanket.
9. Finish the frittata by scattering the crumbled goat cheese over the top.
10. Place the skillet or pie dish in the preheated oven and bake for 20-25 minutes, or until the frittata is set and the top is lightly golden.
11. Take the frittata out of the oven and give it 5 minutes to cool down and set before slicing.
12. Finish off the frittata with a flourish of freshly chopped parsley scattered over the top.
13. Cut the frittata into 6 equal slices and serve warm.

Nutritional breakdown per serving:

Calories: 195 kcal, Protein: 13 grams, Carbohydrates: 8 grams, Fat: 13 grams, Saturated Fat: 5 grams, Cholesterol: 225 milligrams, Sodium: 360 milligrams, Fiber: 2 grams, and Sugar: 4 grams.

BAKED COD WITH MANGO SALSA AND ROASTED BROCCOLI

- Total Cooking Time: 40 minutes
- Prep Time: 20 minutes
- Cook Time: 20 minutes
- Servings: 4

Ingredients:

For the Mango Salsa:

- 1 ripe mango, diced
- 1/2 red onion, finely chopped
- 1 jalapeño, seeded and finely chopped
- 1/4 cup chopped cilantro
- 2 tablespoons lime juice
- 1/4 teaspoon salt
- For the Baked Cod:
- 4 (6-oz) cod fillets
- 2 tablespoons olive oil
- 1 teaspoon paprika
- 1/2 teaspoon garlic powder
- 1/2 teaspoon salt
- 1/4 teaspoon black pepper

For the Roasted Broccoli:

- 1 pound broccoli florets
- 2 tablespoons olive oil
- 1/2 teaspoon salt
- 1/4 teaspoon black pepper

Instructions:

1. Combine the vibrantly diced mango, red onion with a bit of bite, jalapeño for a kick, and fresh cilantro in a medium bowl. Drizzle with zesty lime juice and season with a pinch of salt (1/4 teaspoon) to create a refreshing salsa. Toss well to combine.
2. Pop the oven on to preheat at 400°F (200°C) while you prep the remaining ingredients.

3. Preheat your oven. To save on scrubbing, line a baking sheet with parchment paper or a silicone mat. Then, add the cod fillets.
4. Give the cod a delicious flavor boost by drizzling it with 2 tablespoons of olive oil and sprinkling with paprika, garlic powder, salt (½ teaspoon), and black pepper (¼ teaspoon).
5. Bake the cod for 15-18 minutes, or until it flakes easily with a fork.
6. While the cod cooks, prep the broccoli on another sheet. Drizzle the florets with olive oil (about 2 tablespoons), sprinkle with salt (½ teaspoon), and add a touch of black pepper (¼ teaspoon). Give the broccoli a quick toss with the oil, salt, and pepper. Next, send them to the oven to roast alongside the cod.
7. Roast the broccoli for 15-18 minutes, or until it is tender and lightly browned.
8. Place the baked cod fillets on a serving plate or individual plates.
9. Top each cod fillet with a generous amount of the prepared mango salsa.
10. Serve the roasted broccoli alongside the cod and mango salsa.

Nutritional breakdown per serving:

Calories: 310 kcal, Protein: 32 grams, Carbohydrates: 18 grams, Fat: 13 grams, Saturated Fat: 2 grams, Cholesterol: 60 milligrams, Sodium: 630 milligrams, Fiber: 5 grams, and Sugar: 9 grams.

QUINOA AND KALE STUFFED PORTOBELLO MUSHROOMS

- Total Cooking Time: 45 minutes
- Prep Time: 20 minutes
- Cook Time: 25 minutes
- Servings: 4

Ingredients:

- 4 portobello caps, prepped
- 2 tablespoons olive oil, divided
- 1 cup cooked quinoa
- 1 cup chopped kale, stems removed
- 1/2 cup diced red onion
- 2 cloves garlic, minced
- 1/4 cup crumbled feta cheese
- 2 tablespoons chopped fresh basil
- 1/4 teaspoon salt
- 1/8 teaspoon black pepper

Instructions:

1. Pop the oven on to preheat at 400°F (200°C) while you prep the remaining ingredients.
2. Gently clean the portobello mushroom caps with a damp cloth and remove the stems. Finely chop the stems.
3. Toss the mushroom caps with 1 tablespoon olive oil. Transfer them, gill-side up, to a baking sheet.
4. Bake the mushroom caps for 10 minutes to partially cook them. Remove from the oven and set aside.
5. Get the skillet hot: heat 1 tablespoon olive oil over medium.
6. Add the chopped mushroom stems, diced red onion, and minced garlic. Sauté for 3-4 minutes until the vegetables are softened.
7. Cook the kale for 2-3 minutes, stirring occasionally, until wilted.
8. Let the cooked quinoa cool slightly off the heat. Then, fold in the crumbled feta cheese and chopped basil. Season to taste with salt and pepper.
9. Spoon the quinoa and kale mixture evenly into the partially baked portobello mushroom caps.
10. Pop the stuffed mushrooms back in the oven and bake for another 15-18 minutes. They're done when the mushrooms are tender and the filling is hot and bubbly.

11. Carefully transfer the stuffed portobello mushrooms to a serving plate.
12. Serve the quinoa and kale stuffed portobello mushrooms warm, garnished with additional fresh basil if desired.

Nutritional breakdown per serving:

Calories: 200 kcal, Protein: 10 grams, Carbohydrates: 20 grams, Fat: 10 grams, Saturated Fat: 3 grams, Cholesterol: 15 milligrams, Sodium: 310 milligrams, Fiber: 4 grams, and Sugar: 3 grams.

SUCCULENT SHRIMP AND SWEET PINEAPPLE SKEWERS WITH COLORFUL BELL PEPPERS

- Total Cooking Time: 30 minutes
- Prep Time: 20 minutes
- Cook Time: 10 minutes
- Servings: 4

Ingredients:

- 1 pound large shrimp, peeled and deveined
- 1 fresh pineapple, cut into 1-inch cubes (about 1 cup)
- 1 red pepper, cut 1-inch
- 1 yellow pepper, 1-inch pieces
- 2 tablespoons olive oil
- 2 tablespoons lime juice
- 1 tablespoon honey
- 1 teaspoon chili powder
- 1/2 teaspoon garlic powder
- 1/4 teaspoon salt
- 1/8 teaspoon black pepper

Instructions:

1. Combine the shrimp, cubed pineapple, red and yellow peppers in a large mixing bowl.
2. Whisk together olive oil, lime juice, honey, spices, and salt/pepper for a small-batch dressing.
3. Bathe the shrimp and vegetables in the marinade, making sure to coat them completely.
4. Marinate for 15-20 minutes. Cover and refrigerate the bowl to allow the ingredients to absorb the delicious flavors.
5. Get your grill or grill pan scorching hot! Preheat to medium-high heat.
6. Thread the marinated shrimp, pineapple, and bell pepper pieces onto metal or wooden skewers, alternating the ingredients.
7. Grill the skewers for 4-5 minutes per side, or until the shrimp are opaque and cooked through.
8. Be careful not to overcrowd the grill, and grill the skewers in batches if necessary.
9. Transfer the grilled shrimp skewers to a serving platter.

10. Serve the skewers warm, garnished with any remaining marinade or chopped fresh cilantro, if desired.

Nutritional breakdown per serving:

Calories: 260 kcal, Protein: 24 grams, Carbohydrates: 22 grams, Fat: 8 grams, Saturated Fat: 1 grams, Cholesterol: 170 milligrams, Sodium: 400 milligrams, Fiber: 3 grams, and Sugar: 16 grams.

ROASTED SWEET POTATO AND SPINACH BREAKFAST HASH

- Total Cooking Time: 45 minutes
- Prep Time: 15 minutes
- Cook Time: 30 minutes
- Servings: 4

Ingredients:

- 3 cups diced sweet potato (medium)
- 1 tablespoon olive oil
- 1/2 teaspoon smoked paprika
- 1/4 teaspoon salt
- 1/8 teaspoon black pepper
- 1 tablespoon unsalted butter
- 1 small onion, diced (about 1/2 cup)
- 3 cloves garlic, minced
- 5 ounces fresh spinach, roughly chopped
- 4 large eggs
- 2 tablespoons chopped fresh parsley

Instructions:

1. To commence with the recipe, start by preheating your oven to 400°F (200°C).
2. Coat the diced sweet potatoes in a large bowl with olive oil, smoked paprika, salt, and pepper.
3. Evenly distribute the seasoned sweet potatoes on a baking sheet.
4. Bake the seasoned sweet potatoes for 20-25 minutes, flipping them halfway through, until tender and golden brown.
5. Heat a large skillet over medium heat. Once hot, listen for the happy sizzle of the butter as it melts.
6. Add the diced onion and sauté for 3-4 minutes, until translucent.
7. Let the melted butter sizzle for a minute. The butter should be sizzling happily. Let the minced garlic join the party and toast in the pan, releasing its wonderful fragrance.
8. Watch the vibrant green spinach surrender to the heat. Stir it in occasionally, and within 2-3 minutes, it'll transform into tender, wilted greens.
9. Reunite the roasted sweet potatoes with their wilted spinach and onion companions in the skillet. Give everything a gentle stir to create a harmonious medley.
10. Using a spoon, gently press 4 indentations into the hash mixture. These will be cozy nests for our soon-to-be-cooked eggs.

11. Cover the skillet and listen for the gentle sizzle of the eggs as they cook. After 5 minutes, peek in to see if the whites are set and the yolks are cooked to your preference. Give it a few more minutes if needed for perfectly cooked eggs.
12. Carefully transfer the breakfast hash, including the eggs, to serving plates.
13. Garnish with the chopped fresh parsley.
14. Serve the Roasted Sweet Potato and Spinach Breakfast Hash hot, and enjoy!

Nutritional breakdown per serving:

Calories: 250 kcal, Protein: 10 grams, Carbohydrates: 27 grams, Fat: 12 grams, Saturated Fat: 4 grams, Cholesterol: 215 milligrams, Sodium: 360 milligrams, Fiber: 5 grams, and Sugar: 7 grams.

BAKED FALAFEL WITH CUCUMBER-TOMATO SALAD AND HUMMUS

- Total Cooking Time: 40 minutes
- Prep Time: 20 minutes
- Servings: 4

Ingredients:

Baked Falafel:

- 1 can (15 oz) rinsed chickpeas
- 1/2 cup fresh parsley, chopped
- 1/4 cup fresh cilantro, chopped
- 2 cloves garlic, minced
- 1 tsp ground cumin
- 1 tsp ground coriander
- 1/2 tsp baking soda
- 1/4 tsp cayenne pepper (optional)
- Salt and black pepper to taste
- 1 tbsp olive oil

Cucumber-Tomato Salad:

- 1 cucumber, diced
- 2 tomatoes, diced
- 1/4 red onion, thinly sliced
- 2 tbsp fresh lemon juice
- 1 tbsp olive oil
- 2 tbsp chopped fresh parsley
- Salt and black pepper to taste

Hummus:

- 1 can (15 oz) rinsed chickpeas
- 2 tbsp tahini
- 2 tbsp lemon juice
- 1 clove garlic, minced
- 2 tbsp olive oil
- 2 tbsp water
- Salt and black pepper to taste

Directions:

Baked Falafel:

1. To commence with the recipe, start by preheating your oven to 400°F (200°C).
2. To the food processor: chickpeas, parsley, cilantro, garlic, cumin, coriander, baking soda (optional), cayenne (optional), salt, and pepper. Pulse until the mixture is well-combined but still has some texture.
3. Craft 1-inch falafel balls from the mixture and let them rest on a parchment-lined sheet.
4. Drizzle the falafel balls with the olive oil and gently toss to coat.
5. Bake the falafel for 20-25 minutes, giving them a flip midway for even cooking. You'll know they're perfect when they're crispy and boast a delightful golden brown hue.
6. Cucumber-Tomato Salad:
7. Toss together diced cucumber, juicy tomatoes, and thinly sliced red onion in a medium bowl.
8. Give the salad a refreshing bath with a drizzle of lemon juice and olive oil. Toss to make sure everything gets a delightful coating.
9. Garnish the salad with chopped parsley, and season it to perfection with a sprinkle of salt and black pepper.

Hummus:

1. Load up your food processor with all the hummus essentials: chickpeas, tahini, bright lemon juice, aromatic garlic, smooth olive oil, and a touch of water for creaminess.
2. Whirl the hummus ingredients in your food processor until they're velvety smooth and deliciously creamy. Give the mixture a stir every now and then to help everything blend evenly.
3. Give your hummus a flavor boost! Season it with salt and black pepper to your liking.

To Serve:

1. Place the baked falafel, cucumber-tomato salad, and hummus in separate bowls on the table.
2. Serve the falafel, salad, and hummus together, allowing guests to assemble their own plates.

Nutritional breakdown per serving:

Calories: 376 kcal, Protein: 12 grams, Carbohydrates: 44 grams, Fat: 18 grams, Saturated Fat: 2 grams, Cholesterol: 0 milligrams, Sodium: 470 milligrams, Fiber: 10 grams, and Sugar: 2 grams.

GRILLED TUNA STEAK WITH AVOCADO AND TOMATO SALAD

- Total Cooking Time: 25 minutes
- Prep Time: 15 minutes
- Servings: 4

Ingredients:

Tuna Steak:

- 4 (6 oz) tuna steaks
- 2 tbsp olive oil
- 1 tsp lemon zest
- 1 tbsp lemon juice
- 1 tsp dried oregano
- Salt and black pepper to taste

Avocado and Tomato Salad:

- 2 avocados, diced
- 2 tomatoes, diced
- 1/2 red onion, thinly sliced
- 2 tbsp fresh cilantro, chopped
- 1 tbsp olive oil
- 1 tbsp lime juice
- Salt and black pepper to taste

Directions:

Tuna Steak:

1. Pat tuna steaks dry (paper towels!) and season well with salt and freshly cracked pepper.
2. Whisk together olive oil, lemon zest, juice, and oregano in a bowl. Brush this zesty marinade onto the tuna steaks.
3. Get your grill or grill pan scorching for a perfect sear on those juicy tuna steaks.
4. Grill the tuna steaks for 2-3 minutes a side, until a beautiful sear forms and they reach your desired level of doneness. Avoid overcooking to keep the tuna tender and moist.
5. Transfer the grilled tuna steaks to a plate and let them rest for 5 minutes before serving.

6. Avocado and Tomato Salad:
7. Combine diced avocado, diced tomatoes, and thinly sliced red onion in a bowl. Toss carefully to avoid mushing the avocado.
8. Toss the salsa with a drizzle of olive oil and lime juice. Season it simply with salt and pepper for a fresh and balanced taste.
9. Sprinkle the chopped cilantro over the top.

To Serve:

1. Place a grilled tuna steak on each plate.
2. Top the tuna with the avocado and tomato salad.
3. Serve immediately.

Nutritional breakdown per serving:

Calories: 363 kcal, Protein: 34 grams, Carbohydrates: 12 grams, Fat: 22 grams, Saturated Fat: 3 grams, Cholesterol: 46 milligrams, Sodium: 187 milligrams, Fiber: 6 grams, and Sugar: 5 grams.

LENTIL AND VEGETABLE CURRY WITH CAULIFLOWER RICE

- Total Cooking Time: 45 minutes
- Prep Time: 20 minutes
- Servings: 4

Ingredients:

Lentil and Vegetable Curry:

- 1 cup dry red lentils, rinsed
- 2 cups low-sodium vegetable broth
- 1 tbsp olive oil
- 1 medium onion, diced
- 3 cloves garlic, minced
- 1 tbsp grated fresh ginger
- 1 tsp garam masala
- 1 tsp ground cumin
- 1/2 tsp ground coriander
- 1/4 tsp cayenne pepper
- 1 cup chopped cauliflower florets
- 1 cup cubed sweet potato
- 1 cup chopped green beans
- 1 (14 oz) can diced tomatoes
- 1 (13.5 oz) can full-fat coconut milk
- Salt and black pepper to taste
- Chopped fresh cilantro for garnish

Cauliflower Rice:

- 1 head of cauliflower, cut into florets
- 1 tbsp olive oil
- Salt and black pepper to taste

Directions:

Lentil and Vegetable Curry:

1. In a large saucepan, combine the rinsed red lentils and vegetable broth. After a good boil, reduce heat, cover, and simmer for 15-20 minutes. Patience is key – you want those lentils melt-in-your-mouth tender.

2. Heat oil in a large skillet over medium heat until shimmering. Add diced onion and cook 3-4 minutes, stirring occasionally, until softened and translucent.
3. Release the aromatic flavors of the garlic and ginger by cooking them for 1 minute.
4. Introduce the warm spices - garam masala, cumin, coriander, and cayenne pepper. Give everything a good stir to coat the onions, then cook for 1 minute to toast the spices.
5. Add the chopped cauliflower florets, cubed sweet potato, and green beans. Sauté for 5-7 minutes, until the vegetables are slightly softened.
6. Next, stir in the diced tomatoes with their juices and the coconut milk. Cook, simmering gently, for 10-15 minutes, until the vegetables are tender.
7. Gently fold the cooked lentils into the aromatic curry, creating a beautiful blend. Adjust with salt and pepper to create the flavor you desire.
8. Serve the lentil and vegetable curry over the cauliflower rice, garnished with chopped fresh cilantro.

Cauliflower Rice:

1. Pulse the cauliflower florets in batches in a food processor. Aim for a rice-like texture, with small, even crumbles.
2. Bring your large skillet to medium heat and add olive oil. Heat until shimmering, indicating it's ready for cooking. Give the cauliflower rice a good toss to coat with the hot oil. Season generously with salt and black pepper.
3. Cook the cauliflower rice, stirring occasionally, for 5-7 minutes, until tender and heated through.

Nutritional breakdown per serving:

Calories: 411 kcal, Protein: 16 grams, Carbohydrates: 46 grams, Fat: 20 grams, Saturated Fat: 13 grams, Cholesterol: 0 milligrams, Sodium: 341 milligrams, Fiber: 12 grams, and Sugar: 0 grams.

SEARED SCALLOPS WITH ROASTED BEETS AND ARUGULA SALAD

- Total Cooking Time: 40 minutes
- Prep Time: 15 minutes
- Servings: 4

Ingredients:

- 12 large sea scallops (U10 to U12 size)
- 1 tablespoon olive oil
- 1/2 teaspoon dried thyme
- 1/4 teaspoon garlic powder
- Season with salt and pepper
- 2 medium beets, peeled and cut into wedges
- 1 tablespoon olive oil
- 1/2 teaspoon dried rosemary
- Season with salt and pepper
- 4 cups baby arugula
- 1/4 cup crumbled goat cheese
- 1/4 cup chopped walnuts, toasted (optional)
- 2 tablespoons balsamic vinegar
- 1 tablespoon olive oil
- Season with salt and pepper
- 1/4 cup balsamic vinegar
- 1 tablespoon brown sugar
- 1 tablespoon Dijon mustard

Instructions:

1. Pop your oven on to 400°F (200°C) and quickly line a baking sheet with parchment paper.
2. Toss the beet wedges with olive oil, rosemary, salt, and pepper. Spread the seasoned beets on the prepared baking sheet in a single layer.
3. Place the baking sheet with beets in the preheated oven. Roast for 20-25 minutes, or until the beets are tender-crisp and easily pierced with a fork.
4. Thoroughly pat the sea scallops dry with paper towels to ensure a nice sear. In a shallow dish, whisk together olive oil, thyme, garlic powder, salt, and pepper. Add the scallops to the marinade and toss to coat them evenly. Let them rest for at least 10 minutes, or up to 30 minutes for a more intense flavor.

5. Combine balsamic vinegar, brown sugar, and Dijon mustard in a small saucepan. Whisk everything together until well incorporated. Bring to a simmer: Heat the mixture over medium heat, whisking occasionally, until it simmers gently. Let the glaze simmer, stirring occasionally, for 5-7 minutes. Remove from heat and set aside.
6. Toss the baby arugula, crumbled goat cheese, and toasted walnuts (optional) together in a large bowl.
7. Heat a large skillet over medium-high heat. Add a drizzle of olive oil. Once hot, carefully place the scallops in the pan, sear side down. Sear for 2-3 minutes per side, or until golden brown and cooked through (opaque throughout). Do not overcook, or the scallops will become tough.
8. To assemble the salad, drizzle the arugula with balsamic vinegar and olive oil. Season with salt and pepper to taste. Divide the salad among serving plates. Top each plate with roasted beets and seared scallops. Drizzle with balsamic glaze (if using) and enjoy!

Nutritional breakdown per serving:

Calories: 326 kcal, Protein: 19 grams, Carbohydrates: 19 grams, Fat: 21 grams, Saturated Fat: 4 grams, Cholesterol: 35 milligrams, Sodium: 461 milligrams, Fiber: 5 grams, and Sugar: 3 grams.

CHAPTER 5
DESSETR &
SNACKS

DARK CHOCOLATE AND ALMOND ENERGY BITES

- Total Cooking Time: 20 minutes
- Prep Time: 15 minutes
- Servings: 12 energy bites

Ingredients:

- 1 cup raw almonds
- 1/2 cup rolled oats
- 1/4 cup unsweetened shredded coconut
- 1/4 cup unsweetened cocoa powder
- 1/4 cup honey
- 2 tbsp creamy almond butter
- 1 tsp vanilla extract
- 1/4 tsp sea salt

Directions:

1. Load the food processor with raw almonds. Give them short bursts of pulsing action until they're chopped into small pieces. You want them to have some texture, not become a smooth paste.
2. Toss together the chopped almonds, rolled oats, shredded coconut, and cocoa powder in a medium bowl. Make sure everything is well distributed.
3. In a small bowl, whisk together the honey, almond butter, vanilla extract, and sea salt until smooth.
4. Pour the honey-almond butter mixture into the dry ingredients and stir until well combined.
5. Using a small cookie scoop or your hands, form the mixture into 1-inch balls and place them on a parchment-lined baking sheet.
6. Refrigerate the energy bites for at least 15 minutes to allow them to firm up.

Nutritional breakdown per serving (1 energy bite):

Calories: 118 kcal, Protein: 3 grams, Carbohydrates: 13 grams, Fat: 7 grams, Saturated Fat: 2 grams, Cholesterol: 0 milligrams, Sodium: 53 milligrams, Fiber: 2 grams, and Sugar: 5 grams.

BAKED CINNAMON APPLE CHIPS

- Total Cooking Time: 2 hours 15 minutes
- Prep Time: 15 minutes
- Servings: 4 (about 20 chips per serving)

Ingredients:

- 3 large apples, cored and sliced into 1/8-inch thick rounds (Granny Smith, Honeycrisp, or Fuji work well)
- 1 tbsp ground cinnamon
- 1 tsp ground nutmeg (optional)
- 1 tsp granulated sugar (optional)

Directions:

1. Line two large ones with parchment paper. Meanwhile, preheat your oven to 200°F (95°C).
2. In a large bowl, toss them with ground cinnamon, nutmeg (add this if you like it!), and sugar (use it if desired) until everything is well distributed.
3. Spread the apple slices out on the prepared baking sheets. Make sure they're in a single layer with no crowding, so each slice gets kissed by the heat.
4. Give the apple slices some oven love for 1 hour and 30 minutes. Don't forget to turn them over halfway through so they crisp up uniformly on all sides.
5. After 1 hour and 30 minutes, lower the oven temperature to 170°F (75°C). Give them another 30-45 minutes to finish drying out completely.
6. Take the apple chips out of the oven and give them some time to cool down! Let them sit right on the baking sheets for 10-15 minutes until they're no longer warm.
7. Once cooled, transfer the apple chips to an airtight container or resealable bag for storage.

Nutritional breakdown per serving (about 20 chips):

Calories: 80 kcal, Protein: 0 grams, Carbohydrates: 21 grams, Fat: 0 grams, Saturated Fat: 0 grams, Cholesterol: 0 milligrams, Sodium: 0 milligrams, Fiber: 3 grams, and Sugar: 0 grams.

COCONUT CHIA PUDDING WITH BERRIES

- Total Cooking Time: 4 hours 15 minutes
- Prep Time: 15 minutes
- Servings: 4

Ingredients:

- 1 cup unsweetened coconut milk
- 1/2 cup unsweetened almond milk
- 1/4 cup chia seeds
- 2 tbsp maple syrup
- 1 tsp vanilla extract
- 1/4 tsp ground cinnamon
- 1 cup berries (mixed)
- 2 tbsp toasted unsweetened coconut flakes
- 1 tbsp sliced almonds

Directions:

1. Start building your chia pudding! Combine all the ingredients - coconut milk, almond milk, chia seeds, maple syrup, vanilla extract, and cinnamon - in a medium bowl. Whisk them together until uniform.
2. Refrigerate the covered bowl for 4-24 hours. To ensure a smooth consistency, stir occasionally. As it chills, the mixture will thicken up into a delightful pudding.
3. Divide the coconut chia pudding evenly among 4 serving bowls or glasses.
4. Top each serving with the mixed berries, toasted coconut flakes, and sliced almonds.
5. Serve chilled.

Nutritional breakdown per serving:

Calories: 251 kcal, Protein: 5 grams, Carbohydrates: 26 grams, Fat: 16 grams, Saturated Fat: 10 grams, Cholesterol: 0 milligrams, Sodium: 22 milligrams, Fiber: 9 grams, and Sugar: 1 grams.

GRILLED PEACHES WITH HONEY AND YOGURT

- Total Cooking Time: 25 minutes
- Prep Time: 10 minutes
- Servings: 4

Ingredients:

- 4 ripe peaches, halved and pitted
- 2 tbsp olive oil
- 1/4 cup plain Greek yogurt
- 2 tbsp honey, plus more for drizzling
- 1 tsp vanilla extract
- 1/4 tsp ground cinnamon
- 2 tbsp chopped toasted almonds

Directions:

1. Crank up the heat on your grill or grill pan to medium-high.
2. Brush the exposed flesh with olive oil to help them caramelize.
3. Place the peach halves, cut-side down, on the hot grill. Let them sizzle for 3-4 minutes, or until you see nice grill marks and the peaches soften up a bit.
4. Flip the peach halves and grill for an additional 2-3 minutes, or until they are tender and slightly charred.
5. Once they're beautifully grilled, take the peach halves off the heat and let them sit for a moment.
6. Combine Greek yogurt, 2 tablespoons of honey, and vanilla extract in a small bowl. Stir it well until everything is evenly distributed.
7. Arrange the grilled peach halves on a serving plate and top each one with a dollop of the honey-yogurt mixture.
8. Sprinkle the chopped toasted almonds over the top and drizzle with additional honey, if desired.
9. Serve immediately.

Nutritional breakdown per serving:

Calories: 159 kcal, Protein: 5 grams, Carbohydrates: 22 grams, Fat: 7 grams, Saturated Fat: 1 grams, Cholesterol: 5 milligrams, Sodium: 13 milligrams, Fiber: 2 grams, and Sugar: 5 grams.

AVOCADO AND COCOA MOUSSE

- Total Cooking Time: 20 minutes
- Prep Time: 15 minutes
- Servings: 4

Ingredients:

- 2 avocados, scooped
- 1/4 cup unsweetened cocoa powder
- 1/4 cup maple syrup
- 1/4 cup unsweetened almond milk
- 1 tsp vanilla extract
- 1/4 tsp sea salt
- Shaved dark chocolate or cocoa nibs for garnish (optional)

Directions:

1. Combine the avocado flesh in your food processor with cocoa powder, maple syrup, almond milk, vanilla extract, and sea salt. Blend until perfectly smooth and creamy, pausing occasionally to scrape down the sides for even mixing.
2. Taste and adjust sweetness or cocoa flavor as desired.
3. Divide the avocado mousse evenly among 4 small serving dishes or ramekins.
4. Cover and refrigerate for at least 30 minutes to allow the mousse to set.
5. Serve chilled, garnished with shaved dark chocolate or cocoa nibs, if desired.

Nutritional breakdown per serving:

Calories: 229 kcal, Protein: 3 grams, Carbohydrates: 21 grams, Fat: 16 grams, Saturated Fat: 2 grams, Cholesterol: 0 milligrams, Sodium: 124 milligrams, Fiber: 7 grams, and Sugar: 3 grams.

ROASTED SPICED CHICKPEAS

- Total Cooking Time: 35 minutes
- Prep Time: 10 minutes
- Servings: 4 (about 1/2 cup per serving)

Ingredients:

- 1 (15oz) can chickpeas, drained and rinsed
- 1 tbsp olive oil
- 1 tsp ground cumin
- 1 tsp paprika
- 1/2 tsp garlic powder
- 1/2 tsp chili powder
- 1/4 tsp cayenne pepper (optional, for extra heat)
- 1/2 tsp sea salt

Directions:

1. Line it with parchment paper before preheating your oven to 400°F (200°C).
2. Once rinsed and drained, thoroughly dry them with paper towels or a clean kitchen towel.
3. Combine them in a medium bowl with olive oil, cumin, paprika, garlic powder, chili powder, cayenne pepper (use it if you like some heat!), and sea salt. Toss everything together until the chickpeas are well coated.
4. Scatter the spiced chickpeas over the baking sheet in a single layer. Make sure they have enough space to roast evenly and get crispy!
5. Roast the chickpeas for 20-25 minutes, stirring halfway, until they are crispy and golden brown.
6. Take the baking sheet out of the oven and resist the urge to grab a hot chickpea. Let them cool down for 5-10 minutes before serving.

Nutritional breakdown per serving (about 1/2 cup):

Calories: 134 kcal, Protein: 6 grams, Carbohydrates: 19 grams, Fat: 4 grams, Saturated Fat: 1 grams, Cholesterol: 0 milligrams, Sodium: 413 milligrams, Fiber: 5 grams, and Sugar: 2 grams.

ANTIOXIDANT BERRY SMOOTHIE BOWL

- Total Cooking Time: 10 minutes
- Prep Time: 5 minutes
- Servings: 2

Ingredients:

- 1 cup berries (mixed)
- 1 ripe banana, frozen
- 1/2 cup unsweetened almond milk
- 1/4 cup plain Greek yogurt
- 1 tbsp honey (or maple syrup)
- 1 tsp chia seeds
- 1 tsp ground flaxseed
- 1/2 tsp vanilla extract
- Fresh berries (such as strawberries, blueberries, and raspberries)
- Sliced almonds
- Shredded coconut
- Chia seeds

Directions:

1. In a high-powered blender, combine the frozen mixed berries, frozen banana, almond milk, Greek yogurt, honey, chia seeds, flaxseed, and vanilla extract.
2. Blend the ingredients until smooth and creamy, about 1-2 minutes.
3. Pour the smoothie into two serving bowls.
4. Top each smoothie bowl with the desired toppings, such as fresh berries, sliced almonds, shredded coconut, and additional chia seeds.
5. Serve immediately and enjoy!

Nutritional breakdown per serving:

Calories: 262 kcal, Protein: 9 grams, Carbohydrates: 42 grams, Fat: 8 grams, Saturated Fat: 2 grams, Cholesterol: 5 milligrams, Sodium: 43 milligrams, Fiber: 9 grams, and Sugar: 3 grams.

NO-BAKE WALNUT AND DATE BARS

- Total Cooking Time: 15 minutes
- Prep Time: 10 minutes
- Servings: 12 bars

Ingredients:

- 1 cup raw walnuts
- 1 cup pitted Medjool dates
- 1/2 cup rolled oats
- 2 tbsp unsweetened shredded coconut
- 1 tbsp honey
- 1 tsp vanilla extract
- 1/4 tsp sea salt

Directions:

1. Line an 8x8-inch baking pan with parchment paper. Don't forget to leave some overhang on the sides to lift the whole thing out easily.
2. Process them in a food processor until they have a coarse, grainy texture.
3. Toss the pitted Medjool dates, rolled oats, shredded coconut, honey, vanilla extract, and sea salt into the food processor with the pulsed walnuts. Pulse it all together until it starts to clump and stick together, forming a dough-like consistency.
4. Transfer the date-walnut mixture to your prepared pan. Don't forget the fun part - press it down firmly and evenly with your hands or the back of a spoon. This will pack the mixture in tightly and create a sturdy foundation for your delicious creation.
5. Refrigerate the bars for at least 30 minutes to allow them to firm up.
6. After chilling, use the parchment paper overhang to lift the bars out of the pan like a pro. Cut them into 12 even squares and enjoy!
7. These no-bake walnut and date bars hold onto their freshness for up to a week when stored in an airtight container in the refrigerator. Perfect for keeping healthy and delicious snacks on hand all week long!

Nutritional breakdown per serving:

Calories: 154 kcal, Protein: 3 grams, Carbohydrates: 19 grams, Fat: 9 grams, Saturated Fat: 1 grams, Cholesterol: 0 milligrams, Sodium: 47 milligrams, Fiber: 3 grams, and Sugar: 1 grams.

FROZEN BANANA "NICE CREAM" WITH ALMOND BUTTER

- Total Cooking Time: 10 minutes
- Prep Time: 5 minutes
- Servings: 2

Ingredients:

- 2 ripe bananas, peeled and frozen
- 2 tbsp natural almond butter
- 1/4 cup unsweetened almond milk
- 1 tsp vanilla extract
- 1/4 tsp ground cinnamon (optional)
- Chopped toasted almonds for garnish (optional)

Directions:

1. Kickstart your smoothie! Toss all your ingredients into a high-powered blender or food processor: frozen bananas, almond butter, almond milk, and vanilla extract. Blend it all up for a delicious and refreshing treat.
2. Blend everything together until it's perfectly smooth and creamy. Scrape down sides as needed. If the mixture seems too thick, feel free to add a bit more almond milk for a thinner consistency.
3. If desired, sprinkle in the ground cinnamon and blend briefly to incorporate.
4. Scoop the frozen banana "nice cream" into two serving bowls or glasses.
5. Top the nice cream with chopped toasted almonds, if desired.
6. Serve immediately for a soft-serve delight, or freeze for 30-60 minutes for a classic ice cream texture.

Nutritional breakdown per serving:

Calories: 200 kcal, Protein: 5 grams, Carbohydrates: 25 grams, Fat: 10 grams, Saturated Fat: 1 grams, Cholesterol: 0 milligrams, Sodium: 105 milligrams, Fiber: 4 grams, and Sugar: 2 grams.

BAKED SWEET POTATO FRIES WITH LEMON-GARLIC AIOLI

- Total Cooking Time: 45 minutes
- Prep Time: 15 minutes
- Servings: 4 (about 3/4 cup fries and 2 tbsp aioli per serving)

Ingredients:

Sweet Potato Fries:

- 2 large sweet potatoes, ½-inch fries
- 2 tbsp olive oil
- 1 tsp paprika
- 1/2 tsp garlic powder
- 1/2 tsp sea salt
- 1/2 cup mayonnaise
- 2 tbsp freshly squeezed lemon juice
- 1 garlic clove, minced
- 1/4 tsp Dijon mustard
- 1/4 tsp sea salt
- 1/8 tsp black pepper

Directions:

1. To commence with the recipe, start by preheating your oven to 400°F (200°C). Line two baking sheets with parchment paper.
2. Combine the fries, olive oil, paprika, garlic powder, and sea salt in a large bowl. Make sure everything gets a good coating for flavorful fries in every bite.
3. Lay out the seasoned fries on the baking sheet, making sure none are overlapping.
4. Bake for 25-30 minutes, turning the fries occasionally, until they're crisp and golden brown.
5. In a small bowl, whisk together the mayonnaise, lemon juice, minced garlic, Dijon mustard, sea salt, and black pepper until well combined.
6. Refrigerate the aioli until ready to serve.
7. Arrange the baked sweet potato fries on a serving platter.
8. Serve the lemon-garlic aioli alongside the fries for dipping.

Nutritional breakdown per serving about 3/4 cup fries and 2 tbsp aioli):

Calories: 283 kcal, Protein: 2 grams, Carbohydrates: 27 grams, Fat: 18 grams, Saturated Fat: 3 grams, Cholesterol: 11 milligrams, Sodium: 555 milligrams, Fiber: 4 grams, and Sugar: 1 grams.

BLUEBERRY AND SPINACH SMOOTHIE

- Total Cooking Time: 5 minutes
- Prep Time: 5 minutes
- Servings: 1

Ingredients:

- 1 cup fresh or frozen blueberries
- 1 cup fresh spinach leaves
- 1/2 cup unsweetened almond milk
- 1/2 cup plain Greek yogurt
- 1 tbsp honey (or maple syrup)
- 1 tsp chia seeds
- 1/2 tsp vanilla extract

Directions:

1. In a high-powered blender, combine the blueberries, spinach leaves, almond milk, Greek yogurt, honey, chia seeds, and vanilla extract.
2. Blend the ingredients until smooth and creamy, about 1-2 minutes.
3. Enjoy your smoothie by pouring it into a glass or jar.
4. Enjoy the blueberry and spinach smoothie immediately.

Nutritional breakdown per serving:

Calories: 220 kcal, Protein: 12 grams, Carbohydrates: 35 grams, Fat: 4 grams, Saturated Fat: 1 grams, Cholesterol: 10 milligrams, Sodium: 73 milligrams, Fiber: 6 grams, and Sugar: 0 grams.

DARK CHOCOLATE BARK LOADED WITH ALMONDS AND DRIED CHERRIES

- Total Cooking Time: 30 minutes
- Prep Time: 10 minutes
- Servings: 12 (approximately 2-inch pieces)

Ingredients:

- 8 oz dark chocolate (70% cacao or higher), chopped
- 1/2 cup raw almonds, chopped
- 1/2 cup dried unsweetened cherries, chopped
- 1/4 tsp sea salt

Directions:

1. Line a baking sheet with parchment paper.
2. Using either a double boiler or a heatproof bowl placed over simmering water, melt the chopped dark chocolate, stirring often, until smooth.
3. Once melted, take the chocolate off the heat and fold in the chopped almonds and dried cherries until well combined.
4. On your prepared baking sheet, pour out the chocolate mixture and use a spatula or spoon to spread it into a uniform layer roughly 1/4-inch thick.
5. Gently sprinkle the sea salt flakes evenly across the surface of the chocolate.
6. Refrigerate the chocolate bark for at least 20 minutes, or until it's completely set.
7. Once set, break the bark into 12 irregular pieces.
8. For optimal freshness, store your dark chocolate bark in an airtight container in the refrigerator, where it will keep for up to 2 weeks.

Nutritional breakdown per serving:

Calories: 125 kcal, Protein: 2 grams, Carbohydrates: 11 grams, Fat: 9 grams, Saturated Fat: 4 grams, Cholesterol: 0 milligrams, Sodium: 45 milligrams, Fiber: 2 grams, and Sugar: 2 grams.

ROASTED CINNAMON PEAR CHIPS

- Total Cooking Time: 2 hours
- Prep Time: 15 minutes
- Servings: 12 (approximately 3-4 pear chips per serving)

Ingredients:

- 3 ripe pears, cored and thinly sliced (about 1/8-inch thick)
- 2 tbsp coconut oil, melted
- 2 tsp ground cinnamon
- 1/4 tsp ground nutmeg
- 1/8 tsp sea salt

Directions:

1. To commence with the recipe, start by preheating your oven to 200°F (95°C). Line two baking sheets with parchment paper.
2. In a large bowl, add the pear slices. Drizzle them with the melted coconut oil and then sprinkle with cinnamon, nutmeg, and sea salt. Toss everything together until the pears are evenly coated.
3. Spread the pear slices out in a single, even layer on the prepared baking sheets, leaving space between each slice.
4. Bake the pear chips for 1 to 1.5 hours, flipping them halfway through, until they are dried and crispy.
5. Let the pear chips cool completely on the baking sheets before serving.
6. While room temperature is ideal, you can also store these chips in an airtight container in the refrigerator for up to 2 weeks for extra crispness.

Nutritional breakdown per serving:

Calories: 55 kcal, Protein: 0 grams, Carbohydrates: 8 grams, Fat: 2 grams, Saturated Fat: 2 grams, Cholesterol: 0 milligrams, Sodium: 20 milligrams, Fiber: 2 grams, and Sugar: 0 grams.

MATCHA GREEN TEA CHIA PUDDING

- Total Cooking Time: 2 hours (including chilling time)
- Prep Time: 10 minutes
- Servings: 4 (approximately 1/2 cup per serving)

Ingredients:

- 2 cups unsweetened almond milk
- 1/4 cup chia seeds
- 2 tbsp honey (or maple syrup)
- 2 tsp matcha green tea powder
- 1/2 tsp vanilla extract
- 1/4 tsp ground cinnamon (optional)
- Sliced fresh fruit (such as kiwi, mango, or berries) for topping (optional)

Directions:

1. Create the chia pudding base in a medium bowl. Using a whisk, thoroughly combine the almond milk, chia seeds, honey, vibrant matcha powder, vanilla extract, and a touch of cinnamon (optional) in a medium bowl.
2. Pop the covered bowl in the fridge and stir it occasionally. It needs at least 2 hours to thicken, but for a super thick pudding, you can chill it up to 24 hours.
3. Divide the matcha chia pudding evenly into 4 serving bowls or jars.
4. Top the pudding with sliced fresh fruit, if desired.
5. Serve chilled and enjoy!

Nutritional breakdown per serving:

Calories: 137 kcal, Protein: 4 grams, Carbohydrates: 16 grams, Fat: 6 grams, Saturated Fat: 0 grams, Cholesterol: 0 milligrams, Sodium: 47 milligrams, Fiber: 7 grams, and Sugar: 0 grams.

GRILLED PINEAPPLE SKEWERS WITH HONEY-LIME DRIZZLE

- Total Cooking Time: 20 minutes
- Prep Time: 10 minutes
- Servings: 4

Ingredients:

- 1 ripe pineapple (about 3 lbs)
- 1/2 cup honey
- 1/4 cup fresh lime juice
- 1 tablespoon olive oil
- 1 lime, zested (optional)
- 10 wooden skewers

Detailed Instructions:

1. Soak the wooden skewers in water for at least 10 minutes to prevent burning. Cut the top and bottom off the pineapple. Stand the pineapple upright and cut off the rind, following the curve of the fruit. Discard the rind and core. Cut the pineapple flesh into 1-inch thick cubes.
2. In a small bowl, whisk together the honey, lime juice, and olive oil. Set aside.
3. Thread the pineapple cubes onto the soaked skewers. You can thread them tightly together or leave some space between each cube for even grilling.
4. Preheat it to medium heat, aiming for a temperature around 400°F. Lightly brush the pineapple skewers with olive oil. Once the grill is hot, throw the skewers on! Cook them for 3-4 minutes per side, flipping them occasionally, until they're golden brown and have nice char marks. Brush the skewers generously with the honey-lime drizzle every time you flip them.
5. Once beautifully grilled, transfer the skewers to a plate. For an optional citrus kick, sprinkle with lime zest. Enjoy them warm!

Nutritional breakdown per serving:

Calories: 200 kcal, Protein: 0.5 grams, Carbohydrates: 45 grams, Fat: 2 grams, Saturated Fat: 0 grams, Cholesterol: 0 milligrams, Sodium: 2 milligrams, Fiber: 2 grams, and Sugar: 35 grams.

AVOCADO TOAST WITH SLICED RADISH AND LEMON ZEST

- Total Cooking Time: 10 minutes
- Prep Time: 5 minutes
- Servings: 1

Ingredients:

- 1 slice high-quality bread (sourdough, whole wheat, rye, etc.)
- 1/2 ripe avocado
- 1-2 radishes, thinly sliced
- 1 tablespoon olive oil
- Freshly squeezed lemon juice, to taste
- Season with salt and pepper to taste
- Zest of 1/2 lemon

Detailed Instructions:

1. Heat a pan over medium heat, then swirl in some olive oil to coat. When it's hot, add your bread and cook for a few minutes on each side, until it's golden brown and crispy.
2. Toast your bread over medium heat. As it browns, halve and pit the avocado, scooping the flesh for mashing. Mash the avocado in a small bowl with a fork to your preferred texture - smooth or chunky. Season with lemon juice, salt, and pepper.
3. Slather the toasted bread with the mashed avocado. Pile on thinly sliced radishes, then finish with a generous shower of lemon zest using a fine-grated cheese grater or zester.
4. Give it a final touch with a drizzle of olive oil (optional), then enjoy your creation right away!

Nutritional breakdown per serving:

Calories: 280 kcal, Protein: 4 grams, Carbohydrates: 22 grams, Fat: 18 grams, Saturated Fat: 2 grams, Cholesterol: 10 milligrams, Sodium: 200 milligrams, Fiber: 7 grams, and Sugar: 2 grams.

CUCUMBER SLICES WITH LEMON-DILL HUMMUS

- Total Cooking Time: 15 minutes
- Prep Time: 10 minutes
- Servings: 4

Ingredients:

- 1 can (15 oz) prepared chickpeas
- 1/2 medium cucumber, peeled and chopped
- 1/4 cup fresh dill, chopped (or 1 tablespoon dried dill)
- 2 tablespoons tahini
- 2 tablespoons olive oil
- 1/4 cup lemon juice
- 1 clove garlic, minced
- 1/2 teaspoon salt
- 1/4 teaspoon black pepper
- 1 large English cucumber, thinly sliced
- Fresh dill sprigs, for garnish (optional)

Detailed Instructions:

1. In a food processor or blender, combine the chickpeas, chopped cucumber, dill, tahini, olive oil, lemon juice, garlic, salt, and pepper. Blend until irresistibly smooth and creamy, scraping down the sides occasionally. Feel free to adjust the seasonings to create the perfect flavor profile for you.
2. Wash and dry your English cucumber. Thinly slice it into 1/4-inch rounds, using a mandoline for perfectly uniform slices (or your best knife skills!).
3. Transfer the hummus to a serving bowl. Arrange the cucumber slices around the hummus on a platter. Fresh dill sprigs add a nice touch (optional).

Nutritional breakdown per serving:

Calories: 220 kcal, Protein: 6 grams, Carbohydrates: 22 grams, Fat: 10 grams, Saturated Fat: 2 grams, Cholesterol: 0 milligrams, Sodium: 300 milligrams, Fiber: 5 grams, and Sugar: 4 grams.

BAKED CINNAMON-SUGAR SWEET POTATO FRIES

- Total Cooking Time: 35 minutes
- Prep Time: 15 minutes
- Servings: 4

Ingredients:

- 2 large sweet potatoes (about 1 pound total)
- 1 tablespoon olive oil
- 1/4 cup granulated sugar
- 1 tablespoon ground cinnamon
- 1/2 teaspoon ground nutmeg (optional)
- 1/4 teaspoon salt
- Pinch of cayenne pepper (optional)

Detailed Instructions:

1. To commence with the recipe, start by preheating your oven to 425°F (220°C). Line two baking sheets with parchment paper.
2. Wash and dry the sweet potatoes. Give your sweet potatoes a uniform cut! Aim for fries that are around 1/2 inch thick and 3-4 inches long. Cutting them evenly helps them cook consistently.
3. This phrasing uses a culinary term ("dress") implying a light coating. Toss everything together with your hands or tongs until the fries are well coated.
4. This focuses on the action and clarifies that these are not wet ingredients.
5. This focuses on the fries being coated and avoids mentioning "coated."
6. Bake for 20-25 minutes, turning the fries once during cooking, until they're crisp and golden brown on the outside but still tender in the middle.
7. Once golden brown and tender, transfer the fries to a plate. Give them a couple of minutes to cool down a bit – just enough so you don't burn your tongue! – then dig in and enjoy them warm.

Nutritional breakdown per serving:

Calories: 250 kcal, Protein: 2 grams, Carbohydrates: 40 grams, Fat: 6 grams, Saturated Fat: 1 grams, Cholesterol: 0 milligrams, Sodium: 120 milligrams, Fiber: 4 grams, and Sugar: 18 grams.

BLUEBERRY AND ALMOND PROTEIN SMOOTHIE

- Total Cooking Time: 5 minutes
- Prep Time: 5 minutes
- Servings: 1

Ingredients:

- 1 cup frozen blueberries
- 1/2 cup unsweetened almond milk
- 1/2 banana, frozen or fresh
- 1 tablespoon almond butter
- 1 scoop (around 30g) protein powder (optional)
- 1/4 cup plain Greek yogurt
- 1/4 cup water or additional almond milk (optional, depending on desired thickness)
- Sweeten to taste with honey (optional)

Detailed Instructions:

1. Combine all ingredients in your blender, reserving honey/maple syrup for later (if using).
2. Blend on high for 30-60 seconds, or until desired consistency is reached. If the smoothie is too thick, add water or additional almond milk, a little at a time, until you reach your desired consistency.
3. For extra sweetness, add honey/maple syrup by teaspoons until desired.
4. Get your hands on this refreshing smoothie by pouring it into a glass and enjoying it immediately.

Nutritional breakdown per serving:

Calories: 250 kcal, Protein: 2 grams, Carbohydrates: 35 grams, Fat: 9 grams, Saturated Fat: 3 grams, Cholesterol: 5 milligrams, Sodium: 40 milligrams, Fiber: 4 grams, and Sugar: 10 grams.

NO-BAKE PISTACHIO AND APRICOT ENERGY BARS

- Total Cooking Time: 10 minutes (plus chilling time)
- Prep Time: 5 minutes
- Servings: 10 bars

Ingredients:

- 1 cup rolled oats
- 1/2 cup chopped dried apricots
- 1/2 cup chopped pistachios
- 1/4 cup chopped pitted dates
- 1/4 cup chopped almonds
- 2 tablespoons chia seeds
- 2 tablespoons almond butter
- 2 tablespoons honey
- 1/4 cup unsweetened shredded coconut (optional)

- Pinch of salt

Detailed Instructions:

1. For easy cleanup, line an 8x8 inch baking dish with parchment paper. In a roomy bowl, combine the rolled oats, chopped dried apricots, pistachios, chopped dates, sliced almonds, and chia seeds. Give it all a good toss to distribute the ingredients evenly.
2. In a small saucepan over low heat, melt the almond butter and honey together until smooth. Stir in a pinch of salt.
3. Drizzle the warm almond butter mixture over the dry ingredients in the bowl. Give everything a good stir to ensure all the oats and nuts are evenly coated.
4. Scrape the oat mixture into your lined baking dish. Use a spatula to firmly press it down, creating a compact and even layer.
5. Sprinkle the top of the bars with shredded coconut (if using) for an extra texture and flavor. Seal the dish tightly with plastic wrap and pop it in the fridge. Let it chill for at least 2 hours, or until the bars are completely firm and hold their shape.
6. Chilled and ready to go! Grab the parchment paper overhang and lift the entire granola bar slab out of the pan. Slice it into 10 delicious, evenly sized bars. Stash any leftovers in an airtight container and keep them cool in the fridge - they'll be good for up to a week!

Nutritional breakdown per serving:

Calories: 220 kcal, Protein: 5 grams, Carbohydrates: 28 grams, Fat: 10 grams, Saturated Fat: 4 grams, Cholesterol: 0 milligrams, Sodium: 30 milligrams, Fiber: 5 grams, and Sugar: 15 grams.

BAKED PEAR AND WALNUT CRISP

- Total Cooking Time: 50 minutes
- Prep Time: 15 minutes
- Servings: 6

Ingredients:

- 3 large ripe pears (such as Bosc, Bartlett, or Anjou)
- 2 tablespoons lemon juice
- 1/4 cup water
- 1 cup old-fashioned rolled oats
- 1/2 cup chopped walnuts
- 1/2 cup all-purpose flour
- 1/4 cup brown sugar, packed
- 1/4 cup cold, cubed unsalted butter
- 1/2 teaspoon ground cinnamon
- 1/4 teaspoon ground nutmeg
- Pinch of salt
- Vanilla ice cream or whipped cream

Detailed Instructions:

1. Preheat it to 375°F (190°C). Don't forget to grease your 9x13 inch baking dish for easy cleanup later.
2. Peel them and halve them lengthwise. Carefully core the halves, leaving the bottom attached. To prevent browning, whisk together lemon juice and water in a small bowl. Toss the pear halves in this lemony mixture.
3. In a large bowl, combine the rolled oats, chopped walnuts, flour, brown sugar, cinnamon, nutmeg, and salt. Using a pastry cutter or your fingertips, work the cold butter into the dry ingredients until a crumbly mixture forms. The size of the crumbles should vary, with some larger and some smaller.
4. Fill the baking dish with the pear halves, cut-side down, in a snug single layer. Drizzle the crisp topping evenly over the pears.
5. Bake the crisp for 40-45 minutes, watching for the pears to soften and the topping to turn a delicious golden brown and bubbly.
6. For the best texture, resist digging in right away! Let the crisp cool slightly before serving warm. Spoon on some vanilla ice cream or whipped cream.

Nutritional breakdown per serving:

Calories: 350 kcal, Protein: 4 grams, Carbohydrates: 45 grams, Fat: 15 grams, Saturated Fat: 4 grams, Cholesterol: 25 milligrams, Sodium: 120 milligrams, Fiber: 5 grams, and Sugar: 25 grams.

COCONUT AND LIME CHIA PUDDING WITH MANGO

- Total Cooking Time: 5 minutes (plus overnight chilling)
- Prep Time: 5 minutes
- Servings: 2

Ingredients:

- 1 cup (240ml) full-fat coconut milk
- 1/4 cup (60ml) unsweetened almond milk (or other plant-based milk)
- 1/4 cup (35g) chia seeds
- 1 tablespoon (15ml) pure maple syrup or honey (or more to taste)
- 1/2 lime, zested (about 1 teaspoon)
- 1 ripe mango, peeled and diced

Detailed Instructions:

1. Combine the coconut milk, almond milk, chia seeds, maple syrup, and lime zest in a medium bowl or jar. Whisk it all together until well incorporated.
2. Pop a lid or plastic wrap securely on the bowl or jar. Let it chill in the fridge for at least 6 hours, but ideally overnight. Chilling allows the chia seeds to plump up and thicken the mixture into a pudding.
3. While the chia pudding chills, peel and dice the ripe mango.
4. Once the chia pudding is set, divide it evenly between two serving glasses or bowls. Top each portion with half of the diced mango.
5. Enjoy your coconut and lime chia pudding with mango chilled, straight from the refrigerator.

Nutritional breakdown per serving:

Calories: 350 kcal, Protein: 4 grams, Carbohydrates: 35 grams, Fat: 20 grams, Saturated Fat: 1 grams, Cholesterol: 0 milligrams, Sodium: 20 milligrams, Fiber: 8 grams, and Sugar: 20 grams.

ROASTED SPICED CHICKPEAS WITH PAPRIKA AND CUMIN

- Total Cooking Time: 40 minutes
- Prep Time: 10 minutes
- Servings: 4

Ingredients:

- 1 can (15 oz) chickpeas, rinsed
- 1 tablespoon olive oil
- 1 teaspoon smoked paprika
- 1/2 teaspoon ground cumin
- 1/4 teaspoon garlic powder
- 1/4 teaspoon cayenne pepper (optional, for a spicy kick)
- 1/4 teaspoon salt
- Freshly ground black pepper, to taste

Detailed Instructions:

1. To commence with the recipe, start by preheating your oven to 400°F (200°C). For a mess-free bake, use parchment paper to line your baking sheet.
2. Give the rinsed chickpeas a good pat with a clean kitchen towel. Drying them removes extra moisture, which is key for achieving crispy perfection in the oven.
3. Toss the chickpeas in a large bowl with olive oil, smoked paprika, cumin, garlic powder, and pinches of cayenne pepper (if using), salt, and black pepper. Make sure each chickpea gets a good hug of the flavorful spice mix!
4. Scatter the seasoned chickpeas across your baking sheet, making sure they don't cuddle too much. A single layer is key for even crisping!
5. Bake the chickpeas for 30-35 minutes, stirring occasionally, or until golden brown and crispy. Roasting times can be oven gremlins!
6. Once they're nice and crispy, take the chickpeas out of the oven and let them cool down a bit right on the baking sheet before serving.

Nutritional breakdown per serving:

Calories: 180 kcal, Protein: 8 grams, Carbohydrates: 0 grams, Fat: 6 grams, Saturated Fat: 1 grams, Cholesterol: 0 milligrams, Sodium: 300 milligrams, Fiber: 5 grams, and Sugar: 8 grams.

ANTIOXIDANT BERRY SMOOTHIE BOWL WITH GRANOLA

- Total Cooking Time: 10 minutes
- Prep Time: 5 minutes
- Servings: 1

Ingredients:

- 1 cup frozen mixed berries
- 1/2 banana, frozen or fresh
- 1/2 cup unsweetened almond milk
- 1/4 cup plain Greek yogurt
- 1 tablespoon chia seeds
- 1/4 cup granola (homemade or store-bought)
- 1/4 cup fresh berries
- 1 tablespoon chopped nuts
- 1 tablespoon honey (optional)

Detailed Instructions:

1. In a blender, combine the frozen mixed berries, banana, almond milk, Greek yogurt (if using), and chia seeds. Blend until smooth and creamy. You may need to add a little more milk if the mixture is too thick.
2. Pour the blended smoothie into a bowl.
3. Layer your favorite toppings on top of the smoothie. Here are some suggestions:
4. Sprinkle a generous amount of granola for added texture and crunch.
5. Add a variety of fresh berries for extra sweetness and antioxidants.
6. Sprinkle chopped nuts for a touch of healthy fats and protein.
7. Honey drizzle after cooling is your friend (optional).
8. Enjoy your antioxidant berry smoothie bowl immediately!

Nutritional breakdown per serving:

Calories: 350 kcal, Protein: 10 grams, Carbohydrates: 45 grams, Fat: 10 grams, Saturated Fat: 2 grams, Cholesterol: 5 milligrams, Sodium: 60 milligrams, Fiber: 7 grams, and Sugar: 20 grams.

CHOCOLATE AVOCADO MOUSSE WITH BERRIES

- Total Cooking Time: 15 minutes
- Prep Time: 10 minutes
- Servings: 2

Ingredients:

- 1 ripe avocado, halved, pitted, and peeled
- 1/2 cup unsweetened cocoa powder
- 1/4 cup honey
- 1 tablespoon milk (dairy or plant-based)
- 1 teaspoon vanilla extract
- Pinch of salt
- Fresh berries for garnish (raspberries, blueberries, strawberries)

Detailed Instructions:

1. Combine the avocado, cocoa powder, honey, milk, vanilla extract, and a pinch of salt in your blender or food processor.
2. Crank up the blender to high for 30-60 seconds, or until the mixture turns into a velvety dream. If there are any stubborn bits, pause blending and use a spatula to scrape down the sides before continuing. You want everything perfectly incorporated for the ultimate creamy mousse.
3. Divide the mousse evenly between two serving bowls or glasses. Top each serving with fresh berries of your choice.
4. Enjoy your chocolate avocado mousse immediately!

Nutritional breakdown per serving:

Calories: 320 kcal, Protein: 2 grams, Carbohydrates: 30 grams, Fat: 18 grams, Saturated Fat: 5 grams, Cholesterol: 5 milligrams, Sodium: 30 milligrams, Fiber: 7 grams, and Sugar: 18 grams.

GRILLED PINEAPPLE AND KIWI SKEWERS WITH HONEY

- Total Cooking Time: 20 minutes
- Prep Time: 10 minutes
- Servings: 4

Ingredients:

- 1 ripe pineapple, cut into 1-inch cubes
- 2 kiwis, peeled and cut into 1-inch cubes
- 1 tablespoon olive oil
- 1/4 cup honey
- 1 tablespoon fresh lime juice
- Wooden skewers (soaked in water for at least 10 minutes to prevent burning)

Detailed Instructions:

1. Wash and dry the pineapple and kiwis. Cut the pineapple into 1-inch cubes and the kiwis into 1-inch cubes.
2. Thread the pineapple and kiwi cubes alternately onto the soaked wooden skewers.
3. Pre-heat to medium-high, which is roughly 400°F (200°C).
4. Give the skewers a quick brush with olive oil to help them sizzle! Pop them on the hot grill and cook for 2-3 minutes per side. You're looking for slightly softened fruit with pretty grill marks.
5. While the fruit grills, in a small bowl, whisk together the honey and fresh lime juice.
6. Once they're perfectly cooked, take the skewers off the grill and give them a delicious drizzle with the leftover honey-lime mixture. Enjoy them warm or at room temperature!

Nutritional breakdown per serving:

Calories: 180 kcal, Protein: 1 grams, Carbohydrates: 42 grams, Fat: 2 grams, Saturated Fat: 0 grams, Cholesterol: 0 milligrams, Sodium: 2 milligrams, Fiber: 3 grams, and Sugar: 38 grams.

BAKED CINNAMON APPLE CHIPS WITH GREEK YOGURT

- Total Cooking Time: 1 hour 15 minutes
- Prep Time: 15 minutes
- Servings: 4

Ingredients:

- 3 large apples (such as Gala, Fuji, or Granny Smith)
- 2 tablespoons lemon juice
- 1/4 teaspoon ground cinnamon
- 1 cup plain Greek yogurt
- 1/4 cup pure maple syrup
- 1/2 teaspoon vanilla extract

Detailed Instructions:

1. To commence with the recipe, start by preheating your oven to 225°F (110°C). For a mess-free bake, use parchment paper to line your baking sheet.
2. Then, slice them ultra-thin, aiming for about 1/8 inch thickness. If you have one, a mandoline slicer will make this a breeze and ensure perfectly even slices.
3. Toss them in a large bowl with lemon juice to stop them from turning brown.
4. For a warm and spicy twist, dust the apple slices with ground cinnamon and gently toss them to coat.
5. Create a single, even layer of apple slices on the baking sheets, ensuring no slices overlap.
6. Bake the apple slices for 1 hour, flipping them halfway through with a spatula, or until they are dry and crisp but still slightly flexible.
7. Whip up the yogurt dip while the apples bake! In a small bowl, just whisk together Greek yogurt, maple syrup, and vanilla extract until everything's happy and smooth.
8. Take the apple chips out of the oven and let them cool completely right on the baking sheets. This allows them to achieve maximum crispness as they finish cooling.
9. Serve the cooled apple chips with the vanilla yogurt dip for a delicious and healthy snack.

Nutritional breakdown per serving:

Calories: 280 kcal, Protein: 8 grams, Carbohydrates: 50 grams, Fat: 4 grams, Saturated Fat: 1 grams, Cholesterol: 5 milligrams, Sodium: 60 milligrams, Fiber: 5 grams, and Sugar: 28 grams.

ALMOND AND CACAO NIB ENERGY BITES

- Total Cooking Time: 10 minutes (plus chilling time)
- Prep Time: 5 minutes
- Servings: 10-12 bites

Ingredients:

- 1 cup rolled oats
- 1/2 cup raw almonds
- 1/4 cup chopped pitted dates
- 1/4 cup unsweetened shredded coconut (optional)
- 1/4 cup creamy almond butter
- 2 tablespoons honey or maple syrup
- 2 tablespoons chopped cacao nibs
- Pinch of salt

Detailed Instructions:

1. In a large bowl, gather the rolled oats, almonds for a bit of crunch, chopped dates for sweetness, and the optional shredded coconut for a delightful textural surprise.
2. In a small saucepan over low heat, melt the almond butter and honey or maple syrup together until smooth. Stir in a pinch of salt.
3. Drizzle the warm almond butter mixture over the dry ingredients in the bowl. Fold it in gently using a spatula, making sure everything gets a nice, even coating.
4. Gently fold in the chopped cacao nibs, making sure they are distributed evenly throughout the mixture.
5. Using a spoon or your hands, scoop out the mixture and roll them into balls, forming them into bite-sized pieces. Aim for about 1 to 1 ½ tablespoons of mixture per bite.
6. Place the formed energy bites on a plate lined with parchment paper. Refrigerate for at least 30 minutes, or until firm and set.
7. Once chilled, your almond and cacao nib energy bites are ready to enjoy! For future snacking, store leftover energy bites in an airtight container and refrigerate them. They'll stay fresh and delicious for up to a week.

Nutritional breakdown per serving:

Calories: 200 kcal, Protein: 5 grams, Carbohydrates: 25 grams, Fat: 10 grams, Saturated Fat: 1 grams, Cholesterol: 0 milligrams, Sodium: 30 milligrams, Fiber: 4 grams, and Sugar: 15 grams.

FROZEN BANANA "NICE CREAM" WITH PEANUT BUTTER

- Total Cooking Time: 10 minutes (plus freezing time)
- Prep Time: 5 minutes
- Servings: 2

Ingredients:

- 2 ripe bananas, frozen and sliced (peel and slice before freezing)
- 1 tablespoon creamy peanut butter
- 1 tablespoon unsweetened almond milk (or other plant-based milk)
- 1 tablespoon cocoa powder (optional, for a chocolate peanut butter swirl)
- Pinch of salt

Detailed Instructions:

1. If you haven't already, freeze the peeled and sliced bananas for at least 2-3 hours, or until frozen solid.
2. Combine the peanut butter and almond milk in a small bowl. Whisk the mixture until it's smooth and creamy. For a chocolaty twist, you can add a tablespoon of cocoa powder.
3. Add the frozen banana slices to your high-powered blending machine. Blend the mixture until it's smooth and creamy, like soft serve ice cream. This can take 30-60 seconds on high speed. If the mixture seems stuck, pause blending and use a spatula to scrape down the sides. This will help incorporate any thicker pieces for a smoother blend.
4. While the blender is on low speed, slowly pour in the peanut butter mixture (or chocolate peanut butter mixture). This will create delicious swirls throughout the "nice cream."
5. Pour the blended "nice cream" into bowls and enjoy immediately! The consistency will be soft like soft-serve ice cream. If you prefer a firmer texture, place the "nice cream" in a container and freeze for an additional 30 minutes to 1 hour.

Nutritional breakdown per serving:

Calories: 220 kcal, Protein: 2 grams, Carbohydrates: 28 grams, Fat: 12 grams, Saturated Fat: 1 grams, Cholesterol: 0 milligrams, Sodium: 30 milligrams, Fiber: 4 grams, and Sugar: 14 grams.

CUCUMBER SLICES WITH LEMON-GARLIC TZATZIKI DIP

- Total Cooking Time: 15 minutes (plus chilling time)
- Prep Time: 10 minutes
- Servings: 4

Ingredients:

- 1 cup (240ml) plain Greek yogurt
- 1/2 medium cucumber, grated
- 1 tablespoon fresh lemon juice
- 1 clove garlic, minced
- 1 tablespoon olive oil
- 1/4 teaspoon dried dill
- Pinch of salt
- Freshly ground black pepper, to taste
- 1 large English cucumber, thinly sliced
- Fresh dill sprigs (optional, for garnish)

Detailed Instructions:

1. Wash and dry the English cucumber. To achieve thin, round slices, use a mandoline slicer or carefully cut with a sharp knife.
2. Wash and dry the other half cucumber. Use the grater side of a box grater to grate the cucumber.
3. Toss the grated cucumber in a medium bowl with a sprinkle of salt. Let the grated cucumber sit for 5 minutes. This will help draw out excess moisture.
4. Combine the Greek yogurt, olive oil, lemon juice, minced garlic, dried dill, salt, and black pepper in a separate bowl. Whisk everything together until well incorporated.
5. To remove excess moisture, squeeze the grated cucumber over a bowl using a clean kitchen towel or cheesecloth. This will prevent the dip from becoming watery.
6. Fold the squeezed grated cucumber into the yogurt mixture. Stir gently until everything is well combined.
7. Pop the bowl of tzatziki in the refrigerator, covered with plastic wrap or a lid. Let it chill for at least 30 minutes, ideally longer, to allow the flavors to come together beautifully.
8. Fan the cucumber slices out on a serving platter. Serve the chilled tzatziki dip alongside the cucumber slices, with fresh dill sprigs for garnish (optional).

Nutritional breakdown per serving:

Calories: 80 kcal, Protein: 4 grams, Carbohydrates: 7 grams, Fat: 4 grams, Saturated Fat: 1 grams, Cholesterol: 5 milligrams, Sodium: 180 milligrams, Fiber: 1 grams, and Sugar: 4 grams.

CONCLUSION

The anti-inflammatory diet is an effective method for enhancing overall health and wellness. By focusing on whole, nutrient-dense foods that are rich in anti-inflammatory compounds, this diet can help reduce chronic inflammation, alleviate symptoms of inflammatory conditions, and support the body's natural healing processes.

At the core of the anti-inflammatory diet are foods like fruits, vegetables, whole grains, lean proteins, healthy fats, and anti-inflammatory spices and herbs. These foods offer a rich source of antioxidants, omega-3 fatty acids, fiber, and other valuable nutrients that collaborate to regulate the inflammatory response and sustain a well-balanced immune system.

Adhering to the principles of the anti-inflammatory diet can lead to various advantages, such as a decreased risk of chronic illnesses, enhanced joint and muscle function, improved digestive health, heightened energy levels, and an overall improvement in well-being. The diet's emphasis on whole, minimally processed foods also supports sustainable weight management and promotes a more balanced, nourishing approach to eating.

Incorporating the anti-inflammatory diet into one's lifestyle requires a commitment to mindful food choices, meal planning, and experimentation with new recipes and ingredients. Yet, the potential benefits are substantial, as this nutritional strategy can enable individuals to proactively engage in maintaining their well-being and preventing or managing different inflammatory conditions.

In conclusion, the anti-inflammatory diet is a holistic, evidence-based approach to nutrition that offers a promising path towards improved health and well-being. By adopting the principles of this diet, newcomers can begin a voyage of self-exploration, discover relief from inflammatory symptoms, and develop a greater understanding of the potential of food as a form of medicine.

Made in United States
Troutdale, OR
11/03/2024

24394670R00155